A YEAR
OF
Flowers

A JOURNAL OF
DAILY WISDOM

CHERALYN DARCEY

ROCKPOOL

*For my fellow
'SWAMPIES' Sue,
Cassie, Mandy, Marco,
Woodie, Sue and
Grahame, who make
every day feel as though
it's filled with flowers.*

*SWAMP – Sustainable Wetlands
Agricultural Makers Project – is
a gardening ethnobotanical
dream for our community that
has become a reality thanks to
good, honest people who are
willing to get their hands dirty.*

INTRODUCTION

Welcome, fellow flower lover, to a year of growth, wisdom, support and nature-filled delight. As *A Year of Flowers* unfurls it will reveal a flower associated with each day to learn from and enhance your life.

This is a journal I have wanted for myself, a perpetual diary I could keep for a singular purpose such as a place to expand my thoughts, work on personal growth or as a journal tool for my garden, inspirations or writing. I also wanted a diary I could date myself if I choose to and perhaps start a new one each year or whenever it pleased me. I couldn't find one written in the language of flowers so I wrote this, not only for myself but for all my flower-loving friends.

Within this journal you will find a beautiful vintage botanical image of each flower and its Latin name so there is no mistaking its identity. There is also a short passage to support three keywords that will reveal the character of the flower of the day. Have you ever wondered what your birthday flower or that of those you love and know is? With each daily entry I have shared a short insight into these energies.

Be assured, flower friends, this journal is not a random selection of blossoms.

The knowledge I have gained through decades of research on flowers will ensure that the flowers selected are completely aligned energetically through ethnobotanical aspects; they apply for each day no matter whereabouts in the world you are. Of course, there are other plants and flowers associated with each day and they will share similar aspects, but the ones in this journal will open the conversation of the language of plants, and particularly of flowers, for you.

My wish is that you develop your own deep connection with the language of flowers through daily excursions into this journal of nature wisdom. I cannot wait to hear what you do with your flower year, so please share with me at #ayearofflowers.

Bunches of love,
Cheralyn

JANUARY

1 JANUARY

CANDY-STRIPE CARNATION
Dianthus caryophyllus
Desire, plans, goals

Flower wisdom for today
Begin now.
There will be no better time,
no magical sign or person to wait for.
You are all you need.

Birthday flower: people born under this carnation can be reliable self-starters who get things done if the project fits their passion. Watch out, world, for when they find their lane they aim high and true.

'The past has no power over the present moment.'
ECKHART TOLLE

2 JANUARY

CORNFLOWER
Centaurea cyanus
Agreement, friendship, knowledge

Flower wisdom for today
As you grow and change
true friends will be happy for you.
Fill your life with quality relationships
rather than a cast of many.

Birthday flower: the circles cornflower people make throughout life will help others learn and grow. They are teachers and sharers of knowledge both old and new, along with being very hard and dependable workers.

'Be true to your work, your word, and your friend.'
HENRY DAVID THOREAU

3 JANUARY

SPLENDID PAPHIOPEDILUM
Paphiopedilum insigne
Identity, purpose, subconscious

Flower wisdom for today
You have a purpose that is
entwined with who you are.
What you bring to this world,
no matter its size, is of value.

Birthday flower: those born under this orchid are usually people who
dance to their own tune but readily find a productive way to involve
others. They are unique people with the ability to inspire others.

*'I believe a purpose is something for which one is
responsible; it's not just divinely assigned.'*
MICHAEL J. FOX

4 JANUARY

SNOWDROP
Galanthus nivalis
Hope, renewal, solutions

Flower wisdom for today
Change the scenery
and your choices will expand.
Trying the less obvious way
brings illuminations you may
never have noticed.

Birthday flower: a snowdrop person is always the one to get things started
and is a font of brilliant problem-solving capabilities. They are phoenixes
who can rise out of any situation and with a never say never attitude.

*'No problem can be solved from the same level
of consciousness that created it.'*
ALBERT EINSTEIN

5 JANUARY

TRAVELLER'S JOY
Clematis aristata
Study, safety, ingenuity

Flower wisdom for today
You can study and learn in ways
outside of the classroom or book.
Look for the lessons and ideas
and inspiration along the way.

Birthday flower: people born on this day usually find success in the second
half of their lives. They are protectors, carers and steadfast souls who love
to always be learning without fear of making new goals along the way.

*'Never regard study as a duty, but as the
enviable opportunity to learn.'*
ALBERT EINSTEIN

6 JANUARY

APPLE BLOSSOM
Malus domestica
Love, art, self-care

Flower wisdom for today
A love of self will show in everything
you do. Never pass up the opportunity
to look after yourself and do
what makes you happy.

Birthday flower: creativity and a free spirit shines from those born under
the apple blossom. They are natural helpers who are drawn to healing
modalities, forever encouraging warmth within all around them.

*'Self-care equals success. You're going to be more successful
if you take care of yourself and you're healthy.'*
BETH BEHRS

7 JANUARY

OAK-LEAF GERANIUM
Pelargonium quercifolium
Friendship, purity, fertility

Flower wisdom for today
Who can you call friend today?
Hold them closer and let them know.
We are all alight and glow a little
brighter with the good friends
we invite into our lives.

Birthday flower: these folk will ensure that what has begun will
keep on growing. They are group builders, leaders who ensure
growth and progress, and they handle change well.

'I will not let anyone walk through my mind with their dirty feet.'
MAHATMA GANDHI

8 JANUARY

ALOE
Aloe vera
Renewal, integrity, wisdom

Flower wisdom for today
What will stay and what needs to go? Keep that which creates the avenues of deepest sincerity. Do not fear beginning again or even a complete overhaul of a project.

Birthday flower: those born on this day will be incredibly trustworthy, steadfast and clever. They are policy makers and law keepers and will thrive when given challenges.

'Renewal is not just innovation and change. It is also the process of bringing the results of change into line with our purposes.'
JOHN W. GARDNER

9 JANUARY

HYDRANGEA
Hydrangea macrophylla
Perseverance, devotion, understanding

Flower wisdom for today
What is it that stirs the deepest
parts of your heart? It could be
time to explore your purpose
or find new ways to dedicate to it.
Take extra care to learn all you can.

Birthday flower: people born under hydrangea have the gifts of
determination and grit. Their enthusiasm and dedication are valued
by others, along with their deep emotional intelligence.

....
....
....
....
....
....
....
....
....
....
....
....

*'You may encounter many defeats, but you must not be defeated. In
fact, it may be necessary to encounter the defeats, so you can know
who you are, what you can rise from, how you can still come out of it.'*
MAYA ANGELOU

10 JANUARY

LAVENDER
Lavandula angustifolia
Faith, humility, constancy

Flower wisdom for today
Be fearless in your faith and allow
others the space for theirs.
Nothing can lessen the true path
and divine passion of another.

Birthday flower: people of lavender are gentle souls who gravitate
towards leadership by example. They keep their faith powerful
throughout life by sharing it and are steady, strong, reliable friends.

'A candle loses nothing of its light by lighting another candle.'
JAMES KELLER

11 JANUARY

ICE PLANT
Carpobrotus edulis
Eloquence, openness, uplifting

Flower wisdom for today
Do not be too slow to open up
to new ideas, people and places.
Express yourself clearly and
listen well to the answers that come.

Birthday flower: although there is a side to ice plant people that
can appear distant they are actually awaiting the right time to open.
When they do their spirit is as warm as the midday sun.

'We cannot sow seeds with clenched fists.
To sow we must open our hands.'
ADOLFO PÉREZ ESQUIVEL

12 JANUARY

LEMON BLOSSOM
Citrus limon
Promise, longevity, purification

Flower wisdom for today
Build a strong foundation
and you will find your stability.
Stand in a clear space and
create sections for endurance.

Birthday flower: lemon blossom people find great joy in being of service, and while they are good planners they can be trusted to quickly leap into action. They keep their promises and are very loyal.

....

....

....

....

....

....

....

....

....

....

....

....

....

....

'Purification is but the cleaning of the lamp-glass which hides the light.'
ANNIE BESANT

13 JANUARY

HYSSOP
Hyssopus officinalis
Forgiveness, healing, cleanliness

Flower wisdom for today
Your surroundings
tell a story of who you are.
Are you expressing truly
the real you and where you want to be?

Birthday flower: hyssop people are incredibly goal oriented and autonomous. Self-improvement is a theme that carries them through life, and they are usually good at building wealth.

'Better keep yourself clean and bright; you are the window through which you must see the world.'
GEORGE BERNARD SHAW

14 JANUARY

MEXICAN MARIGOLD
Tagetes erecta
Acceptance, happiness, warmth

Flower wisdom for today
Look for the best in situations
that are presented to you.
Focus on what can be changed
and make each move meaningful.

Birthday flower: an almost indomitable force beats within the
soul of those born under Mexican marigold. They are courageous
and happy and can find the best in most situations.

'Keep love in your heart. A life without it is like a sunless garden when
the flowers are dead. The consciousness of loving and being loved brings
a warmth and a richness to life that nothing else can bring.'
OSCAR WILDE

19

15 JANUARY

YARROW
Achillea millefolium
Courage, relaxation, elegance

Flower wisdom for today
Even as you step back and rest,
do so with a firm purpose.
Determination can be graceful
and calm while still being engaged.

Birthday flower: yarrow people are pleasure seekers who like to fill their lives with little comforts. They are still quick to jump to meet challenges and can be very brave.

'Courage is grace under pressure.'
ERNEST HEMINGWAY

16 JANUARY

ROSEMARY
Rosemarinus officinalis
Remembrance, loyalty, accuracy

Flower wisdom for today
Do not forget what has made
you the person you are today.
Stay true to your purpose
and your unique heritage.

Birthday flower: those born under rosemary are legacy keepers, the family glue
and those who often find themselves surrounded by others seeking guidance
and leadership. Rosemary people are dependable, curious and dutiful.

'What you remember saves you.'
W.S. MERWIN

17 JANUARY

MIGNONETTE
Reseda odorata
Worth, beauty, charm

Flower wisdom for today
This is a day to indulge in beauty
within and without.
A practicality can be found
in that which inspires emotional joy.

Birthday flower: those born under the mignonette flower are beautifully
expressive people who fill the world with all that is lovely. Their pursuits
are usually undertaken with great force and focus on value.

'What we know matters but who we are matters more.'
BRENÉ BROWN

18 JANUARY

SOLOMON'S SEAL
Polygonatum multiflorum
Support, binding, promise

Flower wisdom for today
Supporting others will
bring a lovely tone to the atmosphere
that you may just need right now.
Do not forget your agreements.

Birthday flower: Solomon's seal people are an interesting mix
of fun-loving individuals who remain extremely dedicated to the
serious side of situations. They always keep their word.

'No act of kindness, no matter how small, is ever wasted.'
AESOP

19 JANUARY

PINK PERIWINKLE
Catharanthus roseus
Connection, self-healing, understanding

Flower wisdom for today
Develop a deeper connection
with your body and self.
Put aside negative self-talk
and put energy into self-discovery.

Birthday flower: those born under pink periwinkle are vibrant people who
are usually creative and strong. They enjoy establishing groups and support
networks for others and thrive when asked to use their influence.

*'Life can only be understood backwards;
but it must be lived forwards.'*
SØREN KIERKEGAARD

20 JANUARY

IMPERIAL LILY
Fritillaria imperialis
Evolution, pride, power

Flower wisdom for today
Bask in accomplishments
but also enjoy the journey,
as this is where true
contentment will be found.
Evolve with a happy heart.

Birthday flower: imperial lily people speak their truth and thoughts loudly
and proudly. They can take on the world and usually do so with a wholehearted
approach and resilience that is inspiring to those around them.

....

....

....

....

....

....

....

....

....

....

....

....

'Evolve into the complete person you were intended to be.'
OPRAH WINFREY

21 JANUARY

KANGAROO PAW
Anigozanthos manglesii
Forgiveness, healing, truce

Flower wisdom for today
You honour your growth when
you hold space for others.
Offer a time for others to be heard
and be completely and safely themselves.

Birthday flower: generous, kind and giving are those born under the kangaroo paw. They are healers and diplomats and seekers of a gentler way of achieving while glowing with a radiant inner beauty that others are drawn to.

'Without forgiveness life is governed by an endless cycle of resentment and retaliation.'
ROBERTO ASSAGIOLI

22 JANUARY

COMMON MULLEIN
Verbascum thapsus
Success, strength, comfort

Flower wisdom for today
The little things count.
True and lasting success is created
over seasons and by appreciating
and honouring each step.

Birthday flower: common mullein people adore the creature comforts
of life and can create them anywhere, as they have a deep love of the
natural world. They are usually more attuned to their feelings.

*'Be faithful in small things because it is
in them that your strength lies.'*
MOTHER TERESA

23 JANUARY

DAPHNE
Daphne odora
Honesty, joy, satisfaction

Flower wisdom for today
Is it honest; is it kind; is it helpful?
Listen and align your inner voice
with your actions and thoughts as
what goes on within shows without.

Birthday flower: daphne people are a curious mix of eclectic individualism and scientifically driven seekers of truth. They adore the hard facts as much as the ethereal wonderment of any situation and can always be relied upon for their honesty.

'Being honest may not get you a lot of friends but it'll always get you the right ones.'
JOHN LENNON

24 JANUARY

SAGE
Salvia officinalis
Inner peace, immortality, purification

Flower wisdom for today
If you choose peace cultivating
it is not difficult. Rid yourself of
what you must to make way
for an unblocked path.

Birthday flower: a certain peaceful aura will always surround those born under sage, even in challenging times. It can be felt along with their old-soul wisdom and ability to add a valuable legacy to any undertaking they embark upon.

*'Do not let the behaviour of others
destroy your inner peace.'*
DALAI LAMA

25 JANUARY

FORSYTHIA
Forsythia x *intermedia*
Anticipation, energy, life force

Flower wisdom for today
Give over a day to the revitalisation
of your personal energy.
Bring yourself back into the alignment
that you know suits you.

Birthday flower: forsythia people sparkle with the most interesting light and
are usually extremely multi-talented. They seem almost predestined for success
but are as happy with quiet achievement as they are with glittering lights.

'The energy of the mind is the essence of life.'
ARISTOTLE

26 JANUARY

GOLDEN WATTLE
Acacia pycnantha
Joy, affirmation, optimism

Flower wisdom for today
You have all you need within
to find positivity and answers.
Though times may be challenging,
remember the seasons soon change.

Birthday flower: although they can tend to be rather dramatic, golden
wattle people are supreme confidence boosters. They are a delight to
be around and can easily find the silver lining in any situation.

....

....

....

....

....

....

....

....

....

....

....

*'Sometimes when you're in a dark place you think you've
been buried, but you've actually been planted.'*
CHRISTINE CAINE

27 JANUARY

PINK CABBAGE ROSE
Rosa x *centifolia* 'Muscosa'
Dignity, grace, kindness

Flower wisdom for today
Whatever you are undertaking,
do so with a kind and open heart.
A lightness of being is found in grace.

Birthday flower: pink cabbage rose people maintain a deep and
ever-evolving focus on social responsibility throughout their lives.
They are compassionate at times to a fault and are true.

*'Grace can neither be bought, earned, or won by the
creature. If it could be, it would cease to be grace.'*
ARTHUR W. PINK

28 JANUARY

KING PROTEA
Protea cynaroides
Courage, origin, creation

Flower Wisdom for Today
What would you do differently
with the benefit of hindsight?

Birthday Flower: Like a flame rising, those born under the influence of
the King Protea have the ability to unfold into a bright new day time and
again. They are brave, a little stubborn and possess a creative heart.

'The art of being wise is the art of knowing what to overlook.'
WILLIAM JAMES

29 JANUARY

RED CARNATION
Dianthus caryophyllus
Abundance, compassion, romance

Flower wisdom for today
Speak to yourself with love
and you will become fearless.
Give a little extra affection
to those around you.

Birthday flower: those born under the red carnation are true romantics who love to love. Strong and fearless, they usually find prosperity in life through their interests, and they are passionate people in all aspects of their life.

'You know you're in love when you can't fall asleep because reality is finally better than your dreams.'
DR SEUSS

30 JANUARY

GENTIAN
Gentiana acaulis
Faith, loveliness, gratitude

Flower wisdom for today
Take a moment to embrace
the world with thanks.
Look more deeply at what is
already here with a sense
of true wonderment.

Birthday flower: gentian people are socially conscious and change
makers. They usually hold fast to a faith that carries them through
life and are brilliant organisers and leaders who easily inspire.

*'Faith moves mountains, but you have to keep
pushing while you are praying.'*
HENRY DAVID THOREAU

31 JANUARY

WHITE CAMELLIA
Camellia japonica
Admiration, destiny, excellence

Flower wisdom for today
When you open your eyes
to the possible future
and embrace imperfection
you can find what is truly yours.

Birthday flower: white camellia people are easily admired as they exude a charismatic charm that is genuine and attractive. They are very good with long-term goals and turning plans to action.

'Destiny is no matter of chance. It is a matter of choice. It is not a thing to be waited for, it is a thing to be achieved.'
WILLIAM JENNINGS BRYAN

FEBRUARY

1 FEBRUARY

EVENING PRIMROSE
Oenothera biennis
Soothing, balance, insight

Flower wisdom for today
A light in any darkness
can be found by standing
in a place of balance.
Try to return to centre.

Birthday flower: those born under the evening primrose have a strong female energy and/or connect easily with it. They can seamlessly transform themselves to encourage positive outcomes and possess a lovely emotional warmth.

'A smile's warmth comes from the fire within the heart.'
ANTHONY T. HINCKS

2 FEBRUARY

PLUM BLOSSOM
Prunus mume
Endurance, integrity, nobility

Flower wisdom for today
Stay true and stay the course,
and don't be tempted to lower
your standards or alter your values.
There is hope for those who wait.

Birthday flower: if the plum blossom is your birth flower then
you are a little prouder than most, but you have a high degree of
virtue. The word 'impossible' is not one you entertain at all!

*'Six essential qualities that are the key to success: sincerity,
personal integrity, humility, courtesy, wisdom, charity.'*
DR WILLIAM C. MENNINGER

3 FEBRUARY

BLUE FLAG IRIS
Iris versicolor
Belief, creativity, enjoyment

Flower wisdom for today
There is much that can be found
to help you create more delight
in life if you look a little closer.
Build belief in the possibility
of happiness.

Birthday flower: the blue flag iris as your birth flower means you are usually highly creative and artistic and have a way of making something blissful out of anything. Contentment is a goal that is important to you that generally comes easily.

*'Nothing is really work unless you would
rather be doing something else.'*
J.M. BARRIE

4 FEBRUARY

FOXGLOVE
Digitalis purpurea
Confidence, youth, magic

Flower wisdom for today
Look back on what it was that
inspired you when you were younger,
for there can be found the secrets
of what it is you may need today.

Birthday flower: foxglove people seem to be forever young. They are usually excellent
communicators and easily hold positions of authority, government or command.
Not only are they self-confident, but they also inspire others to be confident.

....

....

....

....

....

....

....

....

....

....

....

....

....

*'Confidence is when you believe in yourself and your abilities, arrogance
is when you think you are better than others and act accordingly.'*
STEWART STAFFORD

5 FEBRUARY

GARDEN HELIOTROPE
Heliotropium arborescens
Devotion, pleasure, faithfulness

Flower wisdom for today
To dedicate yourself to the pursuit
of anything is to believe in
tomorrow and your part in it.
Learn a new skill, or adopt a
new goal for tomorrow.

Birthday flower: those born under garden heliotrope are not just dreamers of a better life but they are incredibly good at devoting themselves to it as long as they don't listen too hard to the naysayers! They are also extremely trustworthy.

'There are no shortcuts to any place worth going.'
BEVERLY SILLS

6 FEBRUARY

PEACH BLOSSOM
Prunus persica
Prosperity, beauty, promises

Flower wisdom for today
Tension can be a binder of energy that
is needed to get something done,
but once released it is a blessing.
You do not always need to
take the hardest road.

Birthday flower: peach blossom people can sometimes appear to have an
almost aggressive energy, but in truth they are simply forthright and live
very much in the moment. They are brilliant at getting things started.

*'Keep every promise you make and only
make promises you can keep.'*
ANTHONY HITT

7 FEBRUARY

GERBERA
Gerbera jamesonii
Appreciation, celebration, cheerfulness

Flower wisdom for today
Create a celebration of just being
only for you and just for today.
Buy yourself flowers or
take yourself somewhere new.

Birthday flower: those born under gerbera can be the happiest of people.
Others gravitate to them and they seem to be able to dispel any small negativity
that arises. Interestingly, they take longer to heal from larger challenges.

....

....

....

....

....

....

....

....

....

....

....

*'We often take for granted the very things
that most deserve our gratitude.'*
CYNTHIA OZICK

8 FEBRUARY

HOYA
Hoya carnosa
Alignment, breakthroughs, consolidation

Flower wisdom for today
Those who are standing
with you through
hard times are the ones
to keep for later when the
sun shines again.

Birthday flower: if hoya is your birth flower you can see things from angles other people miss. You may be good at the patience required to bring lots of small puzzle pieces together and are always a great friend and ally.

'To have a breakthrough, you must consciously connect with the invisible forces that are everywhere around you, urging you to go beyond your old conditioning.'
DEEPAK CHOPRA

9 FEBRUARY

CHICORY
Cichorium intybus
Momentum, release, favours

Flower wisdom for today
It is time to free something from
your life and rid yourself of
a binding placed upon it.
Breathe once again.

Birthday flower: chicory people are certainly impulsive, but they are also very good at directing energy to where it is most needed. They have a knack for moving obstacles and of finding the way forward for those around them.

'If your position is everywhere, your momentum is zero.'
MICHAEL KORDA

1O FEBRUARY

PANSY
Viola tricolor var. *hortensis*
Resonance, inner strength, heart

Flower wisdom for today
Dig deeper into your inner reserves
for the strength you need
but be sure to spend that
energy on true core values.

Birthday flower: if you were born under the pansy you are a healer of hearts,
one whom others turn to for strength and direction out of emotional turmoil.
You are a great teacher and facilitator as long as you look after yourself!

'Let us be grateful to people who make us happy, they are
the charming gardeners who make our souls blossom.'
MARCEL PROUST

FLAMINGO FLOWER
Anthurium scherzerianum
Welcome, thoughtfulness, diligence

Flower wisdom for today
Open the doors, lift the windows
and be ready to welcome in the new
with an openness to what may come.
Think of others a little
more than yourself.

Birthday flower: anthurium as your birth flower means you are very hospitable and kind and love creating a sense of home for all around you. Often hard working, you can also be depended upon to look after the needs of others.

'Be kind, for everyone you meet is fighting a battle.'
PLATO

12 FEBRUARY

FORGET-ME-NOT
Myosotis sylvatica
Remembrance, assertiveness, character

Flower wisdom for today
At the end of this day
what did you learn?
What could you do differently
to develop your true essence?

Birthday flower: those born under forget-me-not are great heritage keepers and legacy creators. They are profound thinkers who are deeply honourable, and are excellent ambassadors of causes who may even make history themselves.

'I care not what others think of what I do, but I care very much about what I think of what I do! That is character!'
THEODORE ROOSEVELT

13 FEBRUARY

BIRD OF PARADISE
Strelitzia reginae
Excellence, magnificence, self-acceptance

Flower wisdom for today
It is time to focus on excellence
rather than choosing what
fits or is easiest.
Take a shot at the moon
and go where it lands.

Birthday flower: not always as they first appear, bird of paradise people are good at revealing only what they want others to see but make no mistake: they are also brilliant at most things they set their minds to and they never hide their inadequacies.

'What lies behind us and what lies before us are tiny matters compared to what lies within us.'
RALPH WALDO EMERSON

14 FEBRUARY

RED ROSE
Rosa spp.
Respect, courage, love

Flower wisdom for today
Slow down to appreciate
the loves and likes
and the caring that flows out of
and into your world and
fill up on the energy.

Birthday flower: red rose people are fiercely passionate lovers, warriors and supporters of causes. They are the ones you want on your team because they will not let anyone down when it truly matters. 'Loving to love' is their creed.

'If we lose love and self-respect for each other, this is how we finally die.'
MAYA ANGELOU

15 FEBRUARY

TANSY
Tanacetum vulgare
Confrontation, accord, immortality

Flower wisdom for today
Facing something that needs
attention can take you places
you would rather not venture.
Maybe it is time to be adventurous.

Birthday flower: tansy people are fighters, warriors and peace makers. They
will bring things to the attention of those who need to know in order to make
tomorrow a better place. Anything they deem unworthy will be swiftly dealt with.

*'The key to immortality is first living
a life worth remembering.'*
BRUCE LEE

16 FEBRUARY

SCENTED BOUVARDIA
Bouvardia longiflora
Longevity, enthusiasm, recovery

Flower wisdom for today
We do not have time for everything
so respect what you have been given.
Rise with eagerness to the task
but allow yourself space for reflection.

Birthday flower: bouvardia indicates people with amazing tenacity and good
long-range planning ability. They can seem to be overdoing it at times but
in fact are balancing things well, and they are cheerleaders for others.

*'Have you ever sensed that our soul
is immortal and never dies?'*
PLATO

17 FEBRUARY

VERONICA
Veronica spicata
Fidelity, development, perception

Flower wisdom for today
Close your eyes and imagine
you are under a waterfall.
It takes you to a place of absolute
clarity as you step out to the world.

Birthday flower: veronica people are highly intuitive and can see things at a slower and more mindful pace than others. They are quick to heal from challenges as they tackle projects, new adventures and relationships with ease.

*'We thrive not when we've done it all, but
when we still have more to do.'*
SARAH LEWIS

18 FEBRUARY

BLUE GUM
Eucalyptus globulus
Healing, serenity, freedom

Flower wisdom for today
You are the one who
controls your will.
You are free; it is just
your method you need to work on.

Birthday flower: if the blue gum is your birth flower you are naturally drawn to a more ethereal approach to life, healing and relationships. You can get easily weighed down by the mundane as freedom is your driving force.

'You can't calm the storm, so stop trying. What you can do is calm yourself. The storm will pass.'
TIMBER HAWKEYE

19 FEBRUARY

HEATHER
Calluna vulgaris
Trust, faith, protection

Flower wisdom for today
What is it you believe in?
Make it your daily exercise
to cast upon your day
what you trust in.

Birthday flower: heather people are generally hopeful and positive of heart and mind. They are wonderful supporters of others and can see the beauty and value in projects and people that might be missed by others.

....

....

....

....

....

....

....

....

....

....

....

....

....

....

'Trust thyself: every heart vibrates to that iron string.'
RALPH WALDO EMERSON

20 FEBRUARY

BABY'S BREATH
Gypsophila paniculata
Purity, innocence, constancy

Flower wisdom for today
Every moment you experience
is an opportunity for a new alignment,
a chance to be whole.

Birthday flower: baby's breath people can hold fast to most things and somehow make the best of any situation. They are honest in opinion and true in their actions while finding the space to expand their goals with ease.

'Love is energy: it can neither be created nor destroyed.
It just is and always will be, giving meaning to life
and direction to goodness. Love will never die.'
BRYCE COURTENAY

21 FEBRUARY

WINDFLOWER
Anemone coronaria
Reciprocation, flexibility, extremes

Flower wisdom for today
Happiness is not a competition,
nor is it a spectator sport.
Try your best to bend
and to stretch your possibilities.

Birthday flower: those born under the energy of the windflower are dreamers, travellers and the 'possibilitarians' of time. They are sometimes mistaken for being off with the clouds, but that is where they find the stuff of happiness and life.

'There is one word that can be the guide for your life – it is the word reciprocity.'
PEARL S. BUCK

22 FEBRUARY

CALLA LILY
Zantedeschia aethiopica
Dignity, self-worth, rejuvenation

Flower wisdom for today
Practise this meditation:
picture yourself as a great
cupped lily standing strong
and assured and ready to accept the new.

Birthday flower: calla lily as your birth flower indicates a sense of pride that can always bring you back to starting things anew while keeping to your values. Calla lily people can physically and emotionally restore anything.

'*Perhaps the earth can teach us, as when everything seems dead and later proves to be alive.*'
PABLO NERUDA

23 FEBRUARY

SEA HOLLY
Eryngium maritimum
Austerity, independence, sternness

Flower wisdom for today
Although all things are connected it is your ability to stay true while weaving the ribbons of living and being that makes you you.

Birthday flower: those born under the sea holly are incredibly courageous and usually do great things alone, but when they team up they are wonderful leaders. They are fiercely competitive but only in what suits their vision and truth.

'You have to do it yourself, no one else will do it for you. You must work out your own salvation.'
CHARLES E. POPPLESTONE

24 FEBRUARY

FLAME LILY
Gloriosa superba
Success, glory, exuberance

Flower wisdom for today
Follow the path of a plant today
from seed to produce and honour
each progression. Where did your meal
or wood chair come from and journey to?

Birthday flower: flame lily people are great entertainers and creatives and are usually
the life of the party. They are very unique, and if not allowed to be themselves they
suffer greatly. Wonderfully warm in heart and soul, they are also incredible fun.

*'And let us remember too that life, in its exuberance, always succeeds in
overflowing the narrow limits within which man thinks he can confine it.'*
JACQUES-YVES COUSTEAU

25 FEBRUARY

HYACINTH
Hyacinthus orientalis
Playfulness, relief, togetherness

Flower wisdom for today
Imagine your haven of
calm and happiness.
Nestle it in your mind so you can
go to it at will and as needed.
Keep this safe harbour open and within.

Birthday flower: hyacinth people like bringing people together and are often sports oriented in action or interest. They love games, groups, learning and, most of all, fun. They can be counted on to help create and maintain projects.

'Laughter is the tonic, the relief, the surcease for pain.'
CHARLIE CHAPLIN

26 FEBRUARY

SWEET VIBURNUM
Viburnum odoratissimum
Boundaries, survival, clarity

Flower wisdom for today
Imagine a hedge that surrounds you.
Every time an unwanted
thought comes along
toss it over the hedge.

Birthday flower: sweet viburnum people are protectors, justice seekers and marvels of survival. They set clear boundaries, and though they may seem a little secretive or withholding they are actually very honourable and trustworthy.

'Daring to set boundaries is about having the courage to love ourselves, even when we risk disappointing others.'
BRENÉ BROWN

27 FEBRUARY

CATTLEYA ORCHID
Cattleya spp.
Uniqueness, desire, respect

Flower wisdom for today
Take each moment as it comes
today for what it is.
Explore the intricacies
to find the sparks of clarity.

Birthday flower: those born under the cattleya orchid are bound to follow a path completely of their own making, though they will encourage others to come along with them. They are intense lovers and can get a little carried away.

'Who you are authentically is alright.'
LAVERNE COX

MARSHMALLOW
Althaea officinalis
Beneficence, maternal energy, cures

Flower wisdom for today
What can you do for another
without anyone knowing?
Extend yourself for no reward
or applause at least once a week.

Birthday flower: marshmallow as your birth flower indicates you are a
born healer, care giver and support figure. Anything you undertake is
usually for the good of all and the betterment of your situation.

'Life's most urgent questions is:
"What are you doing for others?"'
MARTIN LUTHER KING JR

29 FEBRUARY

CRAB CLAW
Heliconia caribaea
Realisation, pride, attention

Flower wisdom for today
You will always give
yourself the best chance
of success if you stop the doubt.
Be unconditional in your self-belief.

Birthday flower: crab claw people are very interesting and often confuse newcomers to their circle with their off-beat approach to things. They can be very insightful and they love working out puzzles and challenges.

*'With realization of one's own potential and self-confidence
in one's ability, one can build a better world.'*
DALAI LAMA

MARCH

1 MARCH

MARCH LILY
Amaryllis belladonna
Nourishment, sensuality, appreciation

Flower wisdom for today
Be a rock in a river.
Sit and close your eyes,
and visualise you are the rock.
Let the river swirl past as it caresses you.

Birthday flower: March lily people are unafraid to bare all in the
pursuit of their goals. They are comfort seekers who make a house or
any space a home and are generous friends, lovers and teachers.

*'Food is not just fuel. Food is about family, food is about community, food
is about identity. And we nourish all those things when we eat well.'*
MICHAEL POLLAN

DAFFODIL
Narcissus pseudonarcissus
Hope, regard, inspiration

Flower wisdom for today
Imagine someone gaining
things they did not have
or are yet to achieve.
There is your place to grow hope.

Birthday flower: those born under the daffodil are inspirational people with much tenacity and joyful hearts. They may at times bury this positivity, sometimes deeply, but it is there. They are usually held in high regard by others.

'Hope is the only bee that makes honey without flowers.'
ROBERT GREEN INGERSOLL

3 MARCH

CHERRY BLOSSOM
Prunus serrulata
Peace, harmony, return

Flower wisdom for today
Imagine a bird holding your most
precious desires in its claws and beak.
Let it fly from you and watch it
go as it may and return on its own.

Birthday flower: cherry blossom people are peace makers who
delight in and find much to fill their world in the service of others,
improving the world in the process. They are deep thinkers who are
gentle in their soul but they can leap when least expected!

*'He who lives in harmony with himself lives
in harmony with the universe.'*
MARCUS AURELIUS

4 MARCH

RED GERANIUM
Pelargonium x hortorum
Love, virility, preference

Flower wisdom for today
You were born a flower bud
and you can open in the
right conditions, but it may
be time to evolve.

Birthday flower: red geranium people are usually energetic and can be full of
passion, and they have a readiness to action ideas that is really something to behold.
What depletes their zest is finding themselves in places they feel unwanted.

'Esteem must be founded on preference: to hold
everyone in high esteem is to esteem nothing.'
MOLIÈRE

WHITE LILAC
Syringa vulgaris
Spirituality, innocence, modesty

Flower wisdom for today
Try pure prayer; it does not
need to be religious based.
Ask in humility and strength
for what it is you want or need.

Birthday flower: those born under the white lilac are easily connected to the spiritual in life. They believe in the ethereal and make good use of this pure strength and faith. They are mostly youthful in attitude for their entire lives.

'The personal life deeply lived always expands into truths beyond itself.'
ANAÏS NIN

6 MARCH

WILD TULIP
Tulipa sprengeri
Desire, reunion, self-improvement

Flower wisdom for today
Live consciously.
Have your desires
but temper them with that
which also nourishes your circle.

Birthday flower: wild tulip as a birth flower indicates a fiery heart that can be a little too impulsive. Those born under this flower are lovers of people, of never letting go and of passion for the sake of passion. They are creative, generous to a fault and warmly earthy to the core.

'Strive not to be a success, but rather to be of value.'
ALBERT EINSTEIN

7 MARCH

POET'S DAFFODIL
Narcissus poeticus
Confidence, self-love, aspiration

Flower wisdom for today
Balance your ideas
with your current abilities.
Set yourself grand goals but
make room for the groundwork.

Birthday flower: those born beneath the poet's daffodil have great faith in themselves and are only shaken occasionally. Real fake it till you make it souls, they actually have the tenacity to see plans through with dedication.

'Breathe. Let go. And remind yourself that this very moment is the only one you know you have for sure.'
OPRAH WINFREY

8 MARCH

BLUE DELPHINIUM
Delphinium elatum
Possibilities, opportunities,
communication

Flower wisdom for today
An ordinary life
that is built on developing
wisdom, strong values and virtue
is still a grand achievement.

Birthday flower: delphinium people are always very good communicators in all forms. They share information, teachings and opportunities with others and are very community minded. They usually take to leadership as well.

....
....
....
....
....
....
....
....
....
....
....
....

'The possibilities are numerous once we decide to act and not react.'
GEORGE BERNARD SHAW

9 MARCH

PEACH BLOSSOM
Prunus persica
Altruism, romance, luck

Flower wisdom for today
Recognise that though a weakness may be different in you than in another, still it is a human weakness and all deserve a measure of kindness.

Birthday flower: peach blossom people are compassionate and open care givers who find it easy to understand others even in entirely different situations than they are in. They are generally lucky and are great romantics.

'Instead of putting others in their place,
put yourself in their place.'
AMISH PROVERB

10 MARCH

SNAPDRAGON
Antirrhinum majus
Perception, apology, grace

Flower wisdom for today
Breathe in the pace of
resting butterfly wings.
Imagine it just there before you:
graceful, slow and forgiving.

Birthday flower: those born under the snapdragon are very intuitive, and they express their emotions easily and accept challenges well. They can be counted on to join in a worthy cause and will do their very best to bring harmony.

'All our knowledge has its origins in our perceptions.'
LEONARDO DA VINCI

11 MARCH

QUEEN ANNE'S LACE
Daucus carota
Sanctuary, awareness, protection

Flower wisdom for today
Stand in the sunlight and see
for yourself the way your shadows
fall from your body in light.

Birthday flower: Queen Anne's lace people are astute to the needs of others and the requirements they need to meet in life to be happy and productive. They seem to be very natural at providing protection and a safe place for everyone.

....

....

....

....

....

....

....

....

....

....

....

*'Everything that irritates us about others can
lead us to an understanding of ourselves.'*
CARL JUNG

12 MARCH

CALENDULA
Calendula officinalis
Contentment, sacredness, cleansing

Flower wisdom for today
The world tree symbol features
branches and roots entwined to
represent endless energy.
Learn by tracing your energy.

Birthday flower: deeply committed to the sacredness of life and to the precious
moments of light, calendula people find contentment easily due to this devotion.
They are filled with gratitude for the everyday and have a great love of nature.

....

....

....

....

....

....

....

....

....

....

....

....

*'Something opens our wings. Something makes boredom and hurt
disappear. Someone fills the cup in front of us: we taste only sacredness.'*
RUMI

13 MARCH

OPIUM POPPY
Papaver somniferum
Loyalty, remembrance, fertility

Flower wisdom for today
There is nothing wrong
with dreaming of more.
You should have all that you
are willing to work for and grow.

Birthday flower: opium poppy people are great dreamers and somewhat magical in their ways. They appear as a connection to the past and a keeper of the future wisdom, and are growers in every sense of the word. They are true in action and deed.

'Loyalty is the strongest glue which makes
a relationship last for a lifetime.'
MARIO PUZO

14 MARCH

BANKSIA
Banksia spp.
Life, enthusiasm, interest

Flower wisdom for today
Write down every true feeling
you experience today
and explore with depth.
How do these empower or disable?

Birthday flower: if you were born under the energy of the banksia you are easily filled with enthusiasm and can engage others in what interests you. You are a natural salesperson and instructor with the gift of likeability.

'The true secret of happiness lies in taking a genuine interest in all the details of daily life.'
WILLIAM MORRIS

15 MARCH

PEAR BLOSSOM
Pyrus communis
Love, comfort, affection

Flower wisdom for today
The reflection you see of
yourself in the eyes of those
who love you unconditionally
is your true self.

Birthday flower: if you are a pear blossom person you are usually loving,
warm and very affectionate. These are traits that you also demand in
others, but you are a true giver and are good at guiding others to love.

*'Never regret anything you have done with a sincere
affection; nothing is lost that is born of the heart.'*
BASIL RATHBONE

16 MARCH

BELLS OF IRELAND
Moluccella laevis
Luck, openness, awareness

Flower wisdom for today
If you choose to focus
on scarcity you will create it.
Try creating your own luck
through dedicated application.

Birthday flower: bells of Ireland people are uplifting and inspiring. Things just seem to come naturally to them but, truth be told, they are hard workers who take well-calculated risks. They are very self-aware from an early age.

'Openness isn't the end. It's the beginning.'
MARGARET HEFFERNAN

17 MARCH

SWEET PEA
Lathyrus odoratus
Responsibility, gratitude, comfort

Flower wisdom for today
When we radiate with the
energy of gratitude
we become part of a
tide that ebbs back towards us.

Birthday flower: those born under the influence of sweet pea are creatures of luxury, lush surroundings and sometimes more than a little decadence. They love to share their comforts and are people with built-in social responsibility.

*'Successful people have a social responsibility to make
the world a better place and not just take from it.'*
CARRIE UNDERWOOD

18 MARCH

WHITE PEONY
Paeonia lactiflora
Resistance, strength, independence

Flower wisdom for today
Just be, as your life will be filled with
the turmoil of resisting what is.
Acceptance can be empowering.

Birthday flower: white peony people have the heart of a lion and the courage
to stand alone when needed. They are independent in most avenues of life
and are good at finding value in even the most discouraging situations.

....

....

....

....

....

....

....

....

....

....

....

'To find yourself, think for yourself.'
SOCRATES

19 MARCH

WHITE LILY
Lilium spp.
Purity, simplicity, truth

Flower wisdom for today
Create a sacred place.
Make it a space that
only allows the seeking of truth
and the growth of uplifting energy.

Birthday flower: the white lily birth flower indicates people of upmost clarity in thought, action and deed. They are usually found in positions of teaching and spiritual guidance and the healing arts. They are forever students themselves.

*'In character, in manner, in style, in all things,
the supreme excellence is simplicity.'*
HENRY WADSWORTH LONGFELLOW

20 MARCH

LOVE-IN-A-MIST
Nigella damascena
Perplexity, emotional clarity, openness

Flower wisdom for today
The river will cleanse and nourish
as it makes its way to the sea.
Note those you pass and
focus on the effect you have on them.

Birthday flower: love-in-a-mist people are a little more complex than most: they are intriguing in their many layers but are very open once they are trusted and respected. A strong feminine quality or easy connection is usual.

'Quiet minds cannot be perplexed or frightened but go on in fortune or misfortune at their own private pace, like a clock during a thunderstorm.'
ROBERT LOUIS STEVENSON

21 MARCH

PERUVIAN LILY
Alstroemeria spp.
Friendship, devotion, good fortune

Flower wisdom for today
Write letters to your closest friends
telling them what they mean to you.
Treasure the response for here
is the glue of relationships.

Birthday flower: Peruvian lily people are usually popular, which is down
to their ease in making friends and maintaining relationships. They have a
high emotional IQ that they flex daily and are long-term goal keepers.

*'With every breath, I plant the seeds of
devotion, I am a farmer of the heart.'*
RUMI

22 MARCH

ST JOHN'S WORT
Hypericum perforatum
Illumination, protection, consciousness

Flower wisdom for today
You are richer than you think;
great wisdom and solutions
lay within you.
Shine your light inwards.

Birthday flower: there is a natural nobility and almost sage-like aura surrounding those born under the influence of St John's wort. They are drawn to the healing arts and to paths such as mental health support and philosophy.

'There are two kinds of light – the glow that illuminates, and the glare that obscures.'
JAMES THURBER

89

23 MARCH

SCOTCH THISTLE
Onopordum acanthium
Integrity, pride, self-respect

Flower wisdom for today
Try meeting yourself for the first time.
Note your first impressions:
are they aligned with your truth?

Birthday flower: Scotch Thistle people are proud, honest and dependable although they can be a little harsh with their opinions at times. They are resilient and love big challenges, and have an amazing endurance that baffles most.

'Real integrity is doing the right thing, knowing that nobody's going to know whether you did it or not.'
OPRAH WINFREY

24 MARCH

WHITE VANDA ORCHID
Vanda spp.
Empathy, sensitivity, regeneration

Flower wisdom for today
In moments of conflict reflect on
the parts that caused you pain.
These are your notes
to personal healing.

Birthday flower: white vanda orchid people are bridge builders and listeners.
They are usually sensitive and have a shyness that is apparent or one they
bury with bravado. They are blessed with the gift of understanding others.

'I got my start by giving myself a start.'
MADAM C.J. WALKER

25 MARCH

BABY BLUE EYES
Nemophila menziesii
Safety, security, openheartedness

Flower wisdom for today
Act as if it already is.
You will subconsciously
work towards the state you believe.
Open your heart and step forward.

Birthday flower: to be born under baby blue eyes is to have a faith in others and in the universe to hold you up as you venture forward. Those with this as their birth flower easily forgive others and trust in the process.

'I've learned that whenever I decide something with an open heart, I usually make the right decision.'
MAYA ANGELOU

26 MARCH

STRAWFLOWER
Xerochrysum bracteatum
Memory, unconditional
love, perseverance

Flower wisdom for today
Imagine yourself in a welcoming
wildwood. The past has grown
the present, and with love and
persistence the future grows.

Birthday flower: strawflower people never forget and never give up. They
are the legacy keepers of their families and projects, and live with a steady
foot on the past and the future while tending lovingly to the now.

*'The progress of the world will call for the
best that all of us have to give.'*
MARY MCLEOD BETHUNE

27 MARCH

BROOM
Genista canariensis
Expression, adaptability, intelligence

Flower wisdom for today
Confidence can be found
when thinking is clear.
By bringing your focus
to your thinking you can clear it.

Birthday flower: those born on the day of broom are usually highly intelligent and have an almost obsession-like connection with a singular theme in their lives. They are self-assured and interesting problem solvers.

'Intelligence is the ability to adapt to change.'
STEPHEN HAWKING

94

28 MARCH

PINK PROTEA
Protea spp.
Presence, self-healing, determination

Flower wisdom for today
Resist temptation.
The easiest way to lose
your way is to give in
to instant gratification.

Birthday flower: pink protea people have the raw grit and courage of all proteas, with a wrapping of deep compassion and the ability to stay focused on the present. They are creative and can seemingly find inspiration anywhere.

'The only person you are destined to become
is the person you decide to be.'
RALPH WALDO EMERSON

29 MARCH

FREESIA
Freesia spp.
Intimacy, thoughtfulness, expectation

Flower wisdom for today
Believe in those around you
and you will find the
intimacy that makes life
all the sweeter.

Birthday flower: those born under the freesia enjoy a fresh and youthful
exterior/heart with a big dash of earthy sensibility. They are the first
to join in and try new things and often easily find opportunities.

*'Modern life is moving faster than the speed
of thought, or thoughtfulness.'*
REBECCA SOLNIT

30 MARCH

VARIEGATED GARDEN TULIP
Tulipa x gesneriana
Consideration, beauty, probability

Flower wisdom for today
Most people are doing
their best or at least trying to.
We all have different measures.

Birthday flower: variegated tulip people are empathetic and sensual and put great energy into love and in getting what they desire. They can be a little narrow in their attention at times as they weigh up their next move with great care.

'Vision with action can change the world.'
J.A. BAKER

31 MARCH

RAFFLESIA
Rafflesia arnoldii
Birth, tenacity, extension

Flower wisdom for today
Multi-tasking is not a skill
that induces mindful clarity.
Take a day to do more by doing less.

Birthday flower: if rafflesia is your birth flower you are a born fighter and leader and will hold on to your causes, positions and beliefs for as long as they will have you! You don't set out to be the boss but that position is often conferred upon you.

'Power is not given to you. You have to take it.'
BEYONCÉ

APRIL

1 APRIL

SHASTA DAISY
Leucanthemum maximum
Integration, stability, sincerity

Flower wisdom for today
Think of a positive word
that describes you.
Write it down; say it aloud.
Live with that word for today.

Birthday flower: shasta daisy people are direct and strongly goal oriented. They possess a natural ability to succeed but it is usually not seen until later in life. They are dependable and cheerful and value friendships very highly.

'The stability we cannot find in the world, we must create within our own persons.'
NATHANIEL BRANDEN

2 APRIL

WISTERIA
Wisteria sinensis
Expansion, honour, longevity

Flower wisdom for today
Try committing to
deepening your involvement
with someone or to something.
Make it a promise.

Birthday flower: if you were born under wisteria you are extremely
hard working and also very giving to others of your time. Well liked by
others, you are full of ideas not only for yourself but also for others.

*'The tiny seed knew that in order to grow, it needed to be dropped
in dirt, covered with darkness, and struggle to reach the light.'*
SANDRA KRING

3 APRIL

RED TULIP
Tulipa spp.
Passion, desire, belief

Flower wisdom for today
Try this mantra if you are stuck:
'I am now holding harmony
for the place I find myself
and all will balance accordingly.'

Birthday flower: red tulip people are romantic, fun and rather lovely to be around. They easily take centre stage but still love being part of a team or group. Changing jobs or roles is a theme that follows them everywhere in life.

'A creative man is motivated by the desire to achieve, not by the desire to beat others.'
AYN RAND

4 APRIL

LILY OF THE VALLEY
Convallaria majalis
Life purpose, happiness, sweetness

Flower wisdom for today
A few questions for today:
Am I true to my purpose?
Am I hiding myself?
Will this align with my happiness?

Birthday flower: those born under lily of the valley can be impulsive, but they are also go-getters who seem to find breakthroughs before others. They are kind in disposition and very animated when engaging with others.

'The mystery of human existence lies not in just staying alive, but in finding something to live for.'
FYODOR DOSTOEVSKY

5 APRIL

WILD HONEYSUCKLE
Lonicera periclymenum
Unity, devotion, confidentiality

Flower wisdom for today
Notice those times today
when you feel a disconnect.
Ask yourself why you feel that way.

Birthday flower: wild honeysuckle people are usually consistent in their thinking and dealings with others and are often extremely self-confident. Seemingly stubborn, this tenacity is actually a sign of their strong dependability.

'Communication is merely an exchange of information,
but connection is an exchange of our humanity.'
SEAN STEPHENSON

6 APRIL

CROCUS
Crocus sativus
Support, innovation, youth

Flower wisdom for today
Support yourself by
consciously not waiting
for the right time, person or place.
Create your inner support system.

Birthday flower: crocus people can be pedantic; however, they are brilliant team workers who are able to draw a bigger picture while tending to the details. Generally they are unusual in personality, but this endears them to most.

'Creativity is thinking up new things.
Innovation is doing new things.'
THEODORE LEVITT

7 APRIL

NASTURTIUM
Tropaeolum majus
Independence, victory, ability

Flower wisdom for today
What is in your incomplete pile?
Sort it out today and give it
a new finish date.
Do, dedicate or delete!

Birthday flower: those with the nasturtium as their birth flower are imaginative people with a strong independent streak. They can be a little impatient and even rebellious, but this makes them wonderful change-makers.

'You can't build a reputation on what you are going to do.'
HENRY FORD

8 APRIL

ALMOND BLOSSOM
Prunus dulcis
Resolution, self-control, vigour

Flower wisdom for today
When did you last feel
you lost your self-control?
What made you regain it?
If not, why is that?

Birthday flower: almond blossom people are extremely mindful of other people to the point of being advocates for others' welfare. They are good in a crisis, brave, clever and a little more emotional than most and can be shy.

'When you rise in the morning, form a resolution to make the day a happy one for a fellow creature.'
SYDNEY SMITH

9 APRIL

COLUMBINE
Aquilegia vulgaris
Constancy, dreams, vision

Flower wisdom for today
Don't get weighed down by
your choices. Your obligations can
change, as can your choices for today.

Birthday flower: the influence of columbine on those born on this day develops
into a strong work ethic and an ability to go above and beyond in all areas of life.
Columbine people are very physical and believe actions speak the loudest.

'Vision is the art of seeing what is invisible to others.'
JONATHAN SWIFT

AMARANTHUS
Amaranthus caudatus
Immortality, retention, involvement

Flower wisdom for today
Share more than 'likes'.
Pull out three of your favourite
books and offer to swap
with three friends for theirs.

Birthday flower: amaranthus people are often fixated on personal goals but are very attentive and true to those they do eventually settle down with. They like to go it alone with most things, though, and can be a little too enthusiastic at times.

....
....
....
....
....
....
....
....
....
....
....
....

'I always wondered why somebody doesn't do something about that. Then I realized I was somebody.'
LILY TOMLIN

11 APRIL

WHITE SWEET WILLIAM
Dianthus barbatus
Valour, momentum, cooperation

Flower wisdom for today
You are the keeper of the flame.
You burn within, and though
your passion should be shared
be mindful it is kept steady
and protected.

Birthday flower: if sweet William is your birthday flower you are usually the mainstay of your family or whatever initiative or workplace you find yourself in. You are very diplomatic and wonderful at bringing people and ideas together.

'A river is easier to channel than to stop.'
BRANDON SANDERSON

12 APRIL

MUSK ROSE
Rosa moschata
Determination, social
awareness, forgiveness

Flower wisdom for today
Today record what
you are saying to yourself.
Reflect on a better conversation,
one that cares for you.

Birthday flower: musk rose people are usually found in the centre of everything. They do love the limelight, but at the same time they have a huge sense of social justice and care deeply for others. They are often very optimistic people.

'Un... someone like you cares a whole awful lot,
n... ng is going to get better. It's not.'
... EUSS, *THE LORAX*

13 APRIL

STRAWBERRY
Fragaria x *ananassa*
Sensuality, fertility, abundance

Flower wisdom for today
What can you share
of yourself today?
Take that vulnerable step
and open up to new possibilities.

Birthday flower: strawberry people are the pioneers of this world who enjoy nothing better than finding their own way to do things. They can be highly private with their personal life while still letting in a favoured few.

'May your choices reflect your hopes, not your fears.'
NELSON MANDELA

14 APRIL

BOUVARDIA
Bouvardia spp.
Tradition, compliments, cure

Flower wisdom for today
Most days you will come across
someone who causes annoyance.
Uncover something pleasant
about them.

Birthday flower: those born under bouvardia have a great respect for tradition,
history and legacy and will both honour and maintain it. They are usually
eloquent speakers who are well liked and easily hold positions of power.

*'Every heart that has beat strong and cheerfully has left a hopeful impulse
behind it in the world and bettered the tradition of mankind.'*
ROBERT LOUIS STEVENSON

15 APRIL

PINK CARNATION
Dianthus caryophyllus
Encouragement, gratitude, influence

Flower wisdom for today
Habits are roadblocks.
Change out a bad habit
for a good habit to give yourself
more chance to stay with your goals.

Birthday flower: if pink carnation is your birth flower you usually enjoy
an organised environment and are extremely practical in your outlook.
Supportive of others, you will step aside when they need you to.

*You leave old habits behind by starting out with the
thought, "I release the need for this in my life."*
WAYNE DYER

16 APRIL

BUTTERCUP
Ranunculus acris
Humility, cheerfulness, financial gain

Flower wisdom for today
When we are too busy living
we are too busy to know ourselves.
Make sure you learn something
new about yourself every day.

Birthday flower: those born under the buttercup are easily the happiest of people. They are community minded and generous and loyal to friends, family and projects they take on. They can be overly empathetic and take on the problems of others too much.

'It is the hopeful, buoyant, cheerful attitude of mind that wins.
Optimism is a success builder, pessimism an achievement killer.'
ORISON SWETT MARDEN

17 APRIL

ARTICHOKE
Cynara scolymus
Emotional strength, grounding, closure

Flower wisdom for today
Describe an accomplishment
you are happy about.
What did you take with
you into the present?

Birthday flower: those born under the influence of the artichoke are usually deeply spiritual or religious. They often start with nothing or in humble surroundings and rise to great heights of power and success.

....

....

....

....

....

....

....

....

....

....

....

'Life will give you whatever experience is most helpful for the evolution of your consciousness. How do you know this is the experience you need? Because this is the experience you are having at the moment.'
ECKHART TOLLE

18 APRIL

POTATO
Solanum tuberosum
Benevolence, fairness, faith

Flower wisdom for today
Sometimes things may
not be unfair but rather
simply different to suit
a purpose that is not yours.

Birthday flower: potato-born people have a great sense of loyalty and honour and of doing what is fair and just for all. They are usually deeply emotional yet have a simple and beautiful grace about them.

'Life is never fair, and perhaps it is a good thing for most of us that it is not.'
OSCAR WILDE

19 APRIL

ORNAMENTAL GINGER
Curcuma cordata
Determination, perception, skill

Flower wisdom for today
Where in your body
do you feel the pulse
of your energy strongest?
Is it serving or reminding you?

Birthday flower: sometimes ornamental ginger people can be controlling almost to detriment, but they are natural-born leaders who others gravitate to for their strong and effective advice and vision. They never give up.

'Pursue one great decisive aim with force and determination.'
CARL VON CLAUSEWITZ

20 APRIL

LADY SLIPPER ORCHID
Cypripedium selligerum
Service, purpose, inspiration

Flower wisdom for today
If you are hesitating over
future plans or events
try to sit with them right now
and then release them or commit.

Birthday flower: if you were born under the influence of lady slipper orchid it indicates a highly developed intuition and potential to dedicate your life to service. You are kind, generous (sometimes overly so) and a little more sensitive than most.

'Travelers, there is no path; paths are made by walking.'
ANTONIO MACHADO

21 APRIL

LADY'S MANTLE
Alchemilla vulgaris
Softness, solace, care

Flower wisdom for today
Explore your anger for a moment:
'The argument I most often have
with my partner is . . .'
What is the self-care message?

Birthday flower: if lady's mantle is your birth flower you are a great
protector of others and anything you deem as being important to your
immediate environment. You enjoy power, justice and creature comforts.

'When we are afraid, everything rustles.'
SOPHOCLES

22 APRIL

TEN WEEKS STOCK
Matthiola incana
Competition, slowing down, affection

Flower wisdom for today
Is it competition
for improvement
or is it for 'provement'?
Train, race and spar with honour.

Birthday flower: those with ten weeks stock as their birth flower can be rather competitive but they are also generally known for being good sports. They are excellent team leaders and often have a huge soft spot for children.

'Try and fail but don't fail to try.'
STEPHEN KAGGWA

23 APRIL

LEUCADENDRON
Leucadendron spp.
Security, sociability, carefulness

Flower wisdom for today
What is it that makes you
feel most safe?
Grow that within so you
may never be without.

Birthday flower: leucadendron as a birth flower means you are a particularly organised person who is generally optimistic, the life of the party and very approachable. You are good at starting and running groups and teaching and in any supervision role.

'The ultimate security is your understanding of reality.'
H. STANLEY JUDD

BLACK-EYED SUSAN
Rudbeckia hirta
Justice, nurturance, impartiality

Flower wisdom for today
Before anything can be nurtured
it must be learned.
Understanding always
comes before genuine care.

Birthday flower: artistic, lovingness and openness are the qualities usually found in black-eyed Susan people, and they often find themselves in positions that involve a lot of problem solving. Career often comes first for them but not before family.

'Never pray for justice, because you might get some.'
MARGARET ATWOOD

25 APRIL

ROSEMARY
Salvia rosmarinus
Dynamism, accuracy, remembrance

Flower wisdom for today
Remember to listen,
remember to hear and
remember to focus on truth,
but always remember to remember.

Birthday flower: rosemary people are dependable in anything they are committed to; their word really is their complete bond. They are mathematical and analytical and employ swift and effective action with great communication.

'There are few things more powerful than a life lived with passionate clarity.'
ERWIN McMANUS

26 APRIL

WHITE RANUNCULUS
Ranunculus spp.
Attractiveness, everlasting
love, commitment

Flower wisdom for today
Forever starts in a singular moment
to bring your goals closer or
bring your passion to life.

Birthday flower: white ranunculus people do their own thing and often against
the tide, but they have a way of being on the right wave when it counts most.
Working with the earth comes naturally to them, as does finding new ideas.

'You are never too old to set another
goal or to dream a new dream.'
C.S. LEWIS

27 APRIL

APRICOT ROSE
Rosa spp.
Admiration, friendship, dedication

Flower wisdom for today
The most important
friendship you will ever make
is the one with yourself.

Birthday flower: apricot rose people are incredibly action oriented although they do not require or seek the spotlight. They are happy to create networks and build strong connections that always progress to meaningful growth.

'A trusting heart will follow only those who truly follow their heart.'
ANTHONY LICCIONE

28 APRIL

GARDEN PEA
Pisum sativum
Communication, dependability, love

Flower wisdom for today
Giving space to the
communication style of another
is to be open to possibilities
of hearing more deeply.

Birthday flower: garden pea people have a great talent for negotiation, wheeling
and dealing along with taking well-calculated risks. Never try to outwait or
outmanoeuvre them as they will always win with their limitless patience!

'It is often merely for an excuse that we say things are impossible.'
FRANÇOIS DE LA ROCHEFOUCAULD

29 APRIL

BOUGAINVILLEA
Bougainvillea glabra
Grace, sociability, protection

Flower wisdom for today
You can go anywhere
but perhaps not everywhere.
Places have their time
as much as people do.

Birthday flower: those born under bougainvillea are usually great ambassadors of whatever they are involved in. They are dependable, well liked and particularly family oriented and have an air of refinement and good taste.

*'The best way to find yourself is to lose
yourself in the service of others.'*
MAHATMA GANDHI

30 APRIL

DAISY
Bellis perennis
Playfulness, protection, happiness

Flower wisdom for today
Extend today beyond
what is easy, what is safe.
Be adventurous with your ideas
as you just may find a new happy place.

Birthday flower: although rather strong in personality, daisy people are optimistic, affectionate and extremely caring of the feelings of others and are champions of true happiness. Their warmth is undeniable, as is their playful nature.

'The secret of your future is hidden in your daily routine.'
MIKE MURDOCK

MAY

1 MAY

MADONNA LILY
Lilium candidum
Healing, secrets, promise

Flower wisdom for today
Create a radio station
inside your heart of music
that supports you.
Play it often.

Birthday flower: Madonna lily people usually have deep serenity that assists them in working through life and relationships in a positive way. They are realists who offer great dedication to and time with plans, goals and challenges.

....

....

....

....

....

....

....

....

....

....

....

....

*'Secrets have a way of making themselves felt,
even before you know there's a secret.'*
JEAN FERRIS

2 MAY

RED RHODODENDRON
Rhododendron spp.
Temperance, truth, observation

Flower wisdom for today
Find a spot outdoors and sit and
focus on one small square.
Consider everything that lives there.

Birthday flower: those born under the influence of red rhododendron have
keen insight and need to take the lead to be comfortable. They are highly
productive truth seekers who generally prefer working with strong values.

'Live truth instead of expressing it.'
ELBERT HUBBARD

3 MAY

TREE PEONY
Paeonia x *suffruticosa*
Good health, temptation, charm

Flower wisdom for today
Adopt a symbol that means
balance and health to you.
Bring it into your life to move
your intentions to action.

Birthday flower: being born under the tree peony will give you a life
focused on health and the healing arts. Happy with the simple things in
life, you seem to be able to create something from almost nothing.

'That man is richest whose pleasures are cheapest.'
HENRY DAVID THOREAU

4 MAY

CROWEA
Crowea saligna
Possibilities, stability, resolution

Flower wisdom for today
Ask yourself what it was
you bought from your childhood
that created your best self.
What did you forget to pack?

Birthday flower: crowea people are generous, warm-hearted souls who can be depended upon to not only offer support but work with others to ensure good outcomes for all. They love people and are usually the heart of most groups.

'I see possibilities in everything. For everything that's taken away, something of greater value has been given.'
MICHAEL J. FOX

5 MAY

PINK DELPHINIUM
Delphinium elatum
Possibility, sureness, new feelings

Flower wisdom for today
A river is fed by and feeds all
it comes upon in its path.
Though the path may change
its course its essence does not.

Birthday flower: pink delphinium people are teachers of higher concepts and scholars of alternate ideas. Often perfectionists, they delight in using their minds to solve problems and offer constructive advice to others.

'You have the power to change your thoughts, and your thoughts have the power to change your life.'
RON WILLINGHAM

6 MAY

TEXAS BLUEBELL
Eustoma grandiflorum
Appreciation, sensitivity, gratitude

Flower wisdom for today
When you practise reverence
gratitude develops.
Today, pause for respect
so that gratitude blossoms.

Birthday flower: Texas bluebell people are gracious folk with a delightful
sensitivity about them. Often highly imaginative, they are drawn to
the arts but also make wonderful parents, guides and coaches.

*'Feeling gratitude and not expressing it is like
wrapping a present and not giving it.'*
WILLIAM ARTHUR WARD

7 MAY

GRAPE HYACINTH
Muscari armeniacum
Release, dignity, assertion

Flower wisdom for today
Write down challenges
you are currently facing.
Write a letter of farewell to each,
then rip it into pieces and dispose of it.

Birthday flower: if you need someone to support you or your cause then grape hyacinth people can be relied upon. These graceful people will find themselves in positions of power and change while also being personally successful.

'If you doubt yourself, then indeed you stand on shaky ground.'
HENRIK IBSEN

8 MAY

CAMPBELL'S MAGNOLIA
Magnolia campbellii
Wisdom, acceptance, change

Flower wisdom for today
Collect a small object
to represent each of the elements.
Display it in your living space
to connect with universal wholeness.

Birthday flower: Campbell's magnolia people can be rather traditional
and uphold old-fashioned values, but they are open to change when
offered intelligent discussion. They are always exceptionally kind.

*'When you accept yourself,
the whole world accepts you.'*
LAOZI

9 MAY

GUELDER ROSE
Viburnum opulus
Sedate, emotions, morality

Flower wisdom for today
Your morals and values
will help set your boundaries.
What does not honour your values?
How are your values compromised?

Birthday flower: those born under the influence of the Guelder rose hold a
high sense of justice and values. They are fighters for what is right and fair and
are especially powerful people, sometimes physically but always inwardly.

....

....

....

....

....

....

....

....

....

....

....

....

'One kind word can warm three winter months.'
JAPANESE PROVERB

10 MAY

LOVAGE
Levisticum officinale
Strength, daring, attractiveness

Flower wisdom for today
What is holding you back?
Sometimes the things you ignore
are those that hold the
most power for you.

Birthday flower: lovage people are happy to work alone, and seem to have luck on their side and a destiny to succeed with most things they attempt. They have a brilliantly clear understanding of their own intuition and are usually very charming.

'Some of us think holding on makes us strong;
but sometimes it is letting go.'
HERMANN HESSE

11 MAY

WILD ROSE
Rosa acicularis
Trust, new direction, imagination

Flower wisdom for today
Give up having the last word.
It will strengthen your self-control
and open new doorways.

Birthday flower: wild rose people have a dedicated focus on what they undertake coupled with a delightfully eccentric imagination. They can be the creative change-makers of the world and can often be outspoken, but they are also deeply caring.

'You are what you believe yourself to be.'
PAULO COELHO

12 MAY

ALPINE BUTTERCUP
Ranunculus alpestris
Self-worth, talent, activity

Flower wisdom for today
When you want to build a house
you do not ask a tailor.
When you want new clothes
you do not ask a builder.

Birthday flower: alpine buttercup people are playful, well-meaning tricksters.
Often leaders in what appears to be a born talent, they find great joy in undertaking
self-study and then creating their own paths and ways of doing things.

'Talent is never static. It's always dying or growing.'
STEPHEN KING

142

13 MAY

COMMON LILAC
Syringa vulgaris
Appeal, divination, naturalness

Flower wisdom for today
If you could change one thing
about your life right now
what would that be?

Birthday flower: common lilac people are those who seem at times to glide through life with great ease, and if they are faced with challenges they can make them into something gainful. They are popular and enjoy their freedom.

'All truly great thoughts are conceived while walking.'
FRIEDRICH NIETZSCHE

14 MAY

YELLOW FLAG IRIS
Iris pseudacorus
Hope, pride, advancement

Flower wisdom for today
Commit to improvement.
Select one personal project and make
choices that will support this every
day for the next fourteen days.

Birthday flower: yellow iris people are driven to seek out and take hold of opportunities. Confident and assured in personality, they are interestingly private in their close personal lives while being open about their work and personal projects.

'Hope is a renewable option: if you run out of it at the end of the day, you get to start over in the morning.'
BARBARA KINGSOLVER

15 MAY

SOLITARY CLEMATIS
Clematis integrifolia
Awakening, focus, dreams

Flower wisdom for today
Identify the places you have
found guiding wisdom.
What can you do to ensure
its continuance for others?

Birthday flower: softly charismatic, immensely likeable and filled with love and
a deep patience for others, those born under solitary clematis are also the quiet
achievers of the world. They seem to have a natural power to get things done.

'To be everywhere is to be nowhere.'
SENECA

16 MAY

OYSTER PLANT
Acanthus mollis
Defiance, expressiveness, rebellion

Flower wisdom for today
Randomly select an image
from a magazine.
Create a story around it
about standing up for yourself.

Birthday flower: those with the oyster plant as their birth flower possess an expressive nature and can be a little left of centre in their dealings and outward appearance although they are greatly admired. They are the rebels of the world.

'If you cannot get rid of the family skeleton,
you may as well make it dance.'
GEORGE BERNARD SHAW

GOLDEN COLUMBINE
Aquilegia chrysantha
Excitement, intensity, eagerness

Flower wisdom for today
If you were to achieve a current goal
how would it feel, taste, smell and look?
Focus on those aspects now
to bring your goals closer.

Birthday flower: golden columbine people have an intensity about them that
either draws others in or can alienate them. They are extremely affectionate
and very trusting, holding their trust as an unshakeable value.

....

....

....

....

....

....

....

....

....

....

....

....

'You may not control all the events that happen to you,
but you can decide not to be reduced by them.'
MAYA ANGELOU

18 MAY

DILL
Anethum graveolens
Commitment, luck, finances

Flower wisdom for today
It's time to make your own luck.
You do not need to follow in
another's footsteps; look at the
goal and make your own way.

Birthday flower: those with dill as their birth flower will find that good luck seems to find them when they need it the most. They are brave and strong in character and very progressive thinkers, and they will hold their position longer than most.

'Be humble, be hungry and always be the hardest worker in the room.'
DWAYNE JOHNSON

19 MAY

HARDY GERANIUM
Geranium bohemicum
security, joy, energy

Flower wisdom for today
Sometimes the greatest joy
can be found in simply stopping.
Pause, just be and cultivate
contentment.

Birthday flower: being born under the hardy geranium indicates people who are brilliant in positions of diplomacy. They are fair and persuasive and make excellent spokespeople for causes or institutions, and they are usually drawn to study.

'Your energy is your currency; spend it wisely.'
BIANCA BASS

20 MAY

RED AZALEA
Rhododendron spp.
Leadership, innovation, romance

Flower wisdom for today
For today note the good
in all situations no matter
how challenging.
What can be learned?

Birthday flower: brilliantly inventive, red azalea people can make something out of anything and have the gift of communication through any medium. They respond well to change and may in fact seek it throughout their lifetime.

'Innovation is creativity with a job to do.'
JOHN EMMERLING

21 MAY

TIGER LILY
Lilium lancifolium
Pride, resurrection, vision

Flower wisdom for today
Go for a walk and find a stick.
Take it home and feel it, smell it,
really see it, listen and tell its story.

Birthday flower: tiger lily energy is confident, inspiring and creative so those born on this day are bold achievers who are exceptionally good at whatever they turn their focus on. They are outwardly happy, bright and charming.

'The greatest gift of the garden is the restoration of the five senses.'
HANNA RION

22 MAY

BUGLE VINE
Calystegia sepium
Openness, communication, persistence

Flower wisdom for today
Make a list of the positive attributes
you can bring to relationships
and situations. Are you
sharing these effectively?

Birthday flower: those born under the influence of bugle vine are tenacious and
industrious and can be depended upon to come up with clever ideas and solutions.
They are ambitious but can be easily distracted by the next shiny new thing.

'Be silent or say something better than silence.'
PYTHAGORAS

23 MAY

PARSLEY
Petroselinum crispum
Entertainment, transmission, winning

Flower wisdom for today
The price of not taking
chances can result in a
debt of regret that is hard to carry.
You may fail but you will be lighter.

Birthday flower: generous, clever and great communicators who are highly
imaginative are born on the day of parsley. They easily find themselves in
the limelight but are happy to turn it on to others who need or deserve it.

'Entertainment is a sacred pursuit when done well.
When done well, it raises the quality of human life.'
MICHAEL CHABON

24 MAY

PETUNIA
Petunia x *atkinsiana*
Priorities, magnification, hopefulness

Flower wisdom for today
It is never too late
to begin believing in yourself.
Focus on what has worked in the past
and give it your full attention.

Birthday flower: petunia people are wonderfully caring and loving, rarely missing an opportunity to boost the energy or meet the needs of others. They are also very sharp in their observations, and their cleverness and positivity are treats.

'Let your hopes not your hurts shape your future.'
ROBERT H. SCHULLER

2 5 MAY

JADE PLANT
Crassula ovata
Prosperity, boldness, intention

Flower wisdom for today
If you need to break away
to be your best then do it.
Sometimes you need to let go
and find a new place to plant yourself.

Birthday flower: jade plant people are honourable and trustworthy beyond doubt. They attract others easily with their warm and affectionate nature while seeming to create a sense of adventure in any project they undertake.

....

....

....

....

....

....

....

....

....

....

....

'We know there is intention and purpose in the universe,
because there is intention and purpose in us.'
GEORGE BERNARD SHAW

26 MAY

FALSE GOAT'S BEARD
Astilbe rubra
Open-heartedness, nurturance, honour

Flower wisdom for today
What is something you have lost
or are missing from your life?
What would change if you found it?

Birthday flower: people born under false goat's beard are dynamic folk who are the secret rebels of society. While being mild mannered on the surface they will surprise you at some point in what appears to be a huge juxtaposition.

'Always be on the lookout for ways to turn a problem into an opportunity for success. Always be on the lookout for ways to nurture your dream.'
LAOZI

27 MAY

SPIDER PLANT
Chlorophytum comosum
Mindfulness, dedication, creativity

Flower wisdom for today
It's time to take an audit of your living space. Create a new positive feeling by changing or introducing something.

Birthday flower: spider plant people are elegant and assured but may appear to be cold. They are exceptionally mindful and are not ones to rush as they like to take their time and focus on decisions and progression.

'Any job very well done that has been carried out by a person who is fully dedicated is always a source of inspiration.'
CARLOS GHOSN

28 MAY

AFRICAN VIOLET
Saintpaulia ionantha
Spirituality, protection, uniqueness

Flower wisdom for today
Write a description of the
relationship you have with yourself.
What is it that you need
to repair or build?

Birthday flower: African violet people are naturally drawn to the spiritual side of life
and, interestingly, are also very adventurous and even thrill seeking. They do well with
change, cope with having to start things from scratch and are rather competitive.

*'You protect your being when you love
yourself better. That's the secret.'*
ISABELLE ADJANI

BUSH LILY
Clivia miniate
Anticipation, expressiveness, belief

Flower wisdom for today
What are your beliefs and
how do they define your life?
If they hold you back,
what would make you change them?

Birthday flower: those born under the influence of the bush lily want it all and they want it now! They are the spark of their circles and are dynamic in all they take on. They are generous but adore being the centre of attention or at least the action.

'Oh, for a life of sensations rather than thoughts!'
JOHN KEATS

30 MAY

COSMOS
Cosmos bipinnatus
Love, coherency, expansion

Flower wisdom for today
Learn to grow by spending time
with new people in fresh situations.
Jump out of your comfort zone.

Birthday flower: cosmos people are clear thinkers who are meticulous in
their planning and execution. They prefer to carry on in their own ways, are
busy folk and can be a little obsessive although they are very dependable.

....
....
....
....
....
....
....
....
....
....
....
....

'Him that I love, I wish to be free – even from me.'
ANNE MORROW LINDBERGH

31 MAY

ORCHID CACTI
Epiphyllum spp.
Receptive, destiny, adaptability

Flower wisdom for today
Reflect on when you
began to learn a new skill
that you now are adept at.
What was that first day like?

Birthday flower: orchid cactus people can turn their hand at almost anything
and have a great love of inspiring others to join them. They make wonderfully
warm group leaders and assistants and always have a firm eye on success.

....

....

....

....

....

....

....

....

....

....

....

'If we can change our thoughts,
we can change the world.'
H.M. TOMLINSON

JUNE

1 JUNE

PERSIAN IRIS
Iris persica
Stability, perception, energetic balance

Flower wisdom for today
When you have been hurt sometimes
you unknowingly use the same weapons
that caused your pain on others.
Look at ways you might end this cycle.

Birthday flower: people born on Persian iris day are generally sociable, good natured and popular. They have a keen sense of curiosity that leads to work in law, science and study. Easily admired, they also love being with people.

'After the game, the king and the pawn go into the same box.'
ITALIAN PROVERB

2 JUNE

POMEGRANATE
Punica granatum
Ambition, inventiveness, perfection

Flower wisdom for today
Adopt your own tree of life by
finding a tree not in your own garden
but one you can take stewardship of.
Care for it and learn together.

Birthday flower: people born under pomegranate are inspirational, clever and expressive. They are adaptable forward thinkers who carry great influence in all the circles they travel in, but most endearing is their fabulous sense of humour.

'There is nothing noble about being superior to some other man. The nobility is in being superior to your previous self.'
HINDU PROVERB

3 JUNE

THRYPTOMENE
Thryptomene saxicola
Hope, wit, reduction

Flower wisdom for today
Think of your worries
sitting inside a balloon.
Burst that balloon today with action
and set all cares free. Let them go.

Birthday flower: those with thryptomene as their birth flower are great
communicators. They are individual in style yet have a passion for
upholding equality, and are non-judgemental, well liked and assertive.

'The creation of a thousand forests is in one acorn.'
RALPH WALDO EMERSON

4 JUNE

WHITE ROSE
Rosa spp.
Protection, honesty, intuition

Flower wisdom for today
A simple life that is lived in honesty
with values that are true and good
is just as important as one filled
with heroic achievements.

Birthday flower: those born under the white rose tend to be lifelong scholars. They
are blessed with minds that are forever searching and learning, then they pass that
wisdom along. They have a deep curiosity for life and can make good leaders.

'Wrong is wrong even if everyone is doing it;
right is right even if no one is doing it.'
AUGUSTINE OF HIPPO

5 JUNE

PURPLE LOOSESTRIFE
Lythrum salicaria
Forgiveness, harmony, brilliance

Flower wisdom for today
To understand with compassion
the weakness you perceive in others
you have to know what is in yourself
that is weak, broken and in need of care.

Birthday flower: those born under the energies of purple loosestrife are versatile and clever. Perhaps their greatest gift is utilising the things other people overlook, especially ideas and opportunities. They are also very energetic.

'Forgiveness doesn't make the other person right; it makes you free.'
STORMIE OMARTIAN

6 JUNE

MEXICAN LOCUST
Robinia neomexicana
Vision, tolerance, receptiveness

Flower wisdom for today
Know when to
be strong,
be right and
be wrong.

Birthday flower: those born under Mexican locust are immensely effective at communicating concepts and inspiring others. They are determined, dedicated and visionary and make excellent role models, parents and presenters.

'He who breathes deepest lives most.'
ELIZABETH BARRETT BROWNING

7 JUNE

HAZEL
Corylus avellana
Peace, reconciliation, charm

Flower wisdom for today
How is it that you are
the most misunderstood?
Why is it that
you think this?

Birthday flower: hazel people are wonderful at bringing people and ideas together. They are charming, can be rather seductive and have a wonderful sense of fun while being instantly recognisable for their great sense of style.

'Reconciliation is a decision that you take in your heart.'
INGRID BETANCOURT

8 JUNE

DAISY BUSH
Olearia semidentata
Studiousness, individualism, duty

Flower wisdom for today
Are there elements
about you that you
wished others knew?
Why don't they?

Birthday flower: those born under the influence of the daisy bush are effective leaders who seem to gravitate easily into positions of power. They are dedicated individuals who speak their minds easily and are very responsible.

'... *study without desire spoils the memory;*
it retains nothing that it takes in.'
LEONARDO DA VINCI

9 JUNE

BLUE POPPY
Meconopsis simplicifolia
Potential, possibilities, insistence

Flower wisdom for today
Can you measure
personal growth?
How do you do that and
how have you grown?

Birthday flower: blue poppy people are energetic and highly motivated and have a willingness to try just about anything. They are strong-willed outsiders with a youthful zest for life and a versatility that carries them through.

'Potential is not an end-point but a capacity to grow and learn.'
EILEEN KENNEDY-MOORE

10 JUNE

CHINA ASTER
Callistephus chinensis
Capability, variety, elegance

Flower wisdom for today
Once a thing is cut
both sides are wounded.
When it is untied
both ends can make a new beginning.

Birthday flower: those born under the China aster have an easy time of knowing themselves. They are goal setters who enjoy trying new things and are the masters of beginning again when something fails.

'You can, you should, and if you are brave enough to start, you will.'
STEPHEN KING

172

11 JUNE

BREADSEED POPPY
Papaver somniferum
Shielding, legacy, regeneration

Flower wisdom for today
Live today and every day
so that your children see the
best they can aspire to be.

Birthday flower: breadseed poppy people are extremely optimistic and are team players who are tenacious at anything they turn their hand to. They have a strong sense of fairness and are happy to join in most things.

'The things you do for yourself are gone when you are gone,
but the things you do for others remain as your legacy.'
N.D. KALU

12 JUNE

COMMON AGRIMONY
Agrimonia eupatoria
Optimism, true feelings, inner harmony

Flower wisdom for today
The most agreeable people
are those who can
disagree without
being disagreeable.

Birthday flower: those born under common agrimony are generous, happy and bright and are encouragers of other people and groups. They are forever learning and jump on all and any opportunities that come their way.

'Joy is not in things. It is in us.'
RICHARD WAGNER

1 3 JUNE

CHAIN OF HEARTS
Ceropegia woodii
Wishes, adventure, romance

Flower wisdom for today
Have a chat with your future self,
the one who learned
and found the way.

Birthday flower: those born under chain of hearts are romantics who easily fall in and out of love, but once the one comes along they are incredibly loyal. They create a wonderful world around them that all are invited to share.

'The great art of life is sensation,
to feel that we exist, even in pain.
LORD BYRON

14 JUNE

GOLDENROD
Solidago spp.
Caution, encouragement, ambition

Flower wisdom for today
Always be good
at doing good.
Take time
for it every day.

Birthday flower: goldenrod individuals are confident, capable and tenacious and have a huge amount of self-belief. They are prone to sharing their strong opinions but do make very effective and charismatic leaders.

'Nothing in life is to be feared. It is only to be understood.'
MARIE CURIE

15 JUNE

MOONWORT
Botrychium lunaria
Fascination, sincerity, cleverness

Flower wisdom for today
To find your inner truth,
practise quietly walking a spiral
pattern from outside to within daily.

Birthday flower: those born under moonwort are attractive in some way that draws others in and they are also very charming in manner. Although they like to get their own way they are usually well liked and know how to make other people feel good.

'Sincerity makes the very least person to be of more value than the most talented hypocrite.'
CHARLES SPURGEON

16 JUNE

OLIVE
Olea europaea
Wisdom, victory, peace

Flower wisdom for today
The learning of peace and wisdom
is found not only in grand
events but also in the
smallest of daily rituals.

Birthday flower: olive people are adventurous dreamers who are very good
at being ahead of trends. They easily create strong community groups,
partnerships and relationships and are great humanitarians and peacemakers.

*'When the power of love overcomes the love
of power the world will know peace.'*
JIMI HENDRIX

17 JUNE

ANGELICA
Angelica archangelica
Inspiration, persuasion, revelation

Flower wisdom for today
What song inspires you?
Write the lyrics down
and explore the feelings
and thoughts each line lights in you.

Birthday flower: angelica-born people are mentors of anyone that crosses their paths and enjoy nothing more than seeing others reach their dreams. They are rather intense and often highly influential and have hearts of gold.

....

....

....

....

....

....

....

....

....

....

....

'To be persuasive we must be believable; to be believable we must be credible; to be credible we must be truthful.'
EDWARD R. MURROW

BALLOON FLOWER
Platycodon grandiflorus
Contentment, boundaries, security

Flower wisdom for today
Mind your space.
Never seek trouble
as it will easily
find you anyway.

Birthday flower: those born on the day of the balloon flower are usually very popular people with a great deal of likeability. They are highly intelligent and deeply sincere and have an easy manner when expressing their views.

'I am neither of the East nor of the West, no boundaries exist within my breast.'
RUMI

19 JUNE

BITTER ASH
Quassia amara
Purging, involvement, resolution

Flower wisdom for today
What does your
punctuality or lack of it
mean to you and what does
it say about you?

Birthday flower: people born under bitter ash are quick to rise to any task,
argument or situation and will easily inspire others to join them. They are good
at peace making and have no problem in creating lasting legacies of change.

'When I let go of what I am, I become what I might be.'
LAOZI

20 JUNE

WHITE DELPHINIUM
Delphinium elatum
Fierceness, charisma, gain

Flower wisdom for today
Those who are thought of
as being good with people
have the ability to make space
for the journeys of others.

Birthday flower: being born under the influence of the white delphinium
indicates people who are the life of the party and know how to get what they
want from life. They are brilliant communicators and work well with others.

....

....

....

....

....

....

....

....

....

....

....

....

*'Continue. Be loving and be strong. Be fierce and
be kind. And don't give in and don't give up.'*
MAYA ANGELOU

21 JUNE

WOODLAND STRAWBERRY
Fragaria vesca
Certainty, sensuality, acceptance

Flower wisdom for today
Though you may live with a belief
not all will agree with it.
They have not risen in the
same light but in that of their own.

Birthday flower: despite being rather intense, woodland strawberry people are able to let their light-hearted sides shine through. They are determined and pride themselves on their ability to get things done and done well.

'No person is your friend who demands your silence or denies your right to grow.'
ALICE WALKER

22 JUNE

ROMAN CHAMOMILE
Anthemis nobilis
Release, romance, serenity

Flower wisdom for today
Do all your personal truths
serve you well?
Let go of the non-serving
to make room for enlightenment.

Birthday flower: Roman chamomile people strongly believe that new beginnings are always within their capacity. They are imaginative and creative romantics with boundless energy for those within their inner circle.

'Everything passes, nothing remains. Understand this, loosen your grip and find serenity.'
SURYA DAS

23 JUNE

BORAGE
Borago officinalis
Directness, magnetism, courage

Flower wisdom for today
Make a pact
to finish something
you have left undone.
'This month I will...'

Birthday flower: if you want something fixed ask someone born under the influence of borage. They are not only physically handy but make effective negotiators, peacemakers and instructors while always maintaining a great understanding of others.

'I believe that there is a subtle magnetism in Nature, which, if we unconsciously yield to it, will direct us aright.'
HENRY DAVID THOREAU

24 JUNE

HERB BENNET
Geum urbanum
Self-support, skill, talent

Flower wisdom for today
What do you need to hear today
from yourself or others, and
why do you need to hear it?

Birthday flower:: herb Bennet people are extremely independent and become masters of any passion they decide to focus on. They are very good with money, managing all types of resources. and can easily inspire others with their example.

'Allow yourself to be a beginner. No
one starts off being excellent.'
WENDY FLYNN

25 JUNE

ANNUAL HONESTY
Lunaria annua
Abundance, potential, sensitivity

Flower wisdom for today
The measure of activity
has nothing to do
with the amount
of success.

Birthday flower: those born under annual honesty are problem solvers of great capacity and have a keen ability for deep insight. They are sensitive and incredibly empathetic and are able to always find creative solutions for others.

'The greatest crime is not developing your potential. When you do what you do best, you are helping not only yourself, but the world.'
ROGER WILLIAMS

26 JUNE

WHITE AZALEA
Rhododendron spp.
Transition, stamina, staying true

Flower wisdom for today
Every hour today stop and reflect
on what your intention is.
Are you aligned and, if not, why?

Birthday flower: white azalea people possess formidable fortitude and a
love of life that sees them through anything. They are great forces of energy,
leadership and social sensitivity that make them effective community leaders.

*'There is a time for departure even when
there is no certain place to go.'*
TENNESSEE WILLIAMS

27 JUNE

QUEEN OF THE ALPS
Eryngium alpinum
Boundaries, satisfaction, radiating

Flower wisdom for today
What is your favourite
indulgence or treat,
and can you remember
when you discovered it?

Birthday flower: those born under the influence of queen of the alps are
great protectors, organisers and creators of much-needed resources. They are
self-reliant, driven people who love to be front and centre of the action.

*'Learning how to be still, to be really still and let life
happen – that stillness becomes radiance.'*
MORGAN FREEMAN

28 JUNE

AGAPANTHUS
Agapanthus africanus
Stimulation, abundance, potential

Flower wisdom for today
Leave what
has been done
and focus on what
needs to be done.

Birthday flower: opportunities seem to find agapanthus people and they take hold of them quickly. They have a keen eye for the unusual and love nothing more than making something out of nothing while always retaining their uplifting nature.

....

....

....

....

....

....

....

....

....

....

....

....

'The more you see yourself as what you'd like to become, and act as if what you want is already there, the more you'll activate those dormant forces that will collaborate to transform your dream into your reality.'
WAYNE DYER

FOUR O'CLOCK
Mirabilis jalapa
Dreams, timidity, wonder

Flower wisdom for today
There are many paths
to realising your dreams
but only one will
feed your soul as you travel.

Birthday flower: four o'clock people are very good at communicating with others and understanding their positions and needs. They are youthful in spirit and usually appearance and have lively imaginations and energy to boot.

'Curiosity is a delicate little plant that, aside from stimulation, stands mainly in need of freedom.'
ALBERT EINSTEIN

30 JUNE

PLUMBAGO
Plumbago auriculata
Autonomy, motivation, vitality

Flower wisdom for today
Each night before bed
write down an expectation
you have for the following day.
This assists focus and motivation.

Birthday flower: with their love of doing things their way and by themselves, plumbago people can seem a little aloof at first but in fact they are just a little slower to open up to others. They are highly motivated people who love mystery.

'Vitality shows in not only the ability to persist but the ability to start over.'
F. SCOTT FITZGERALD

JULY

1 JULY

GYMEA LILY
Doryanthes excelsa
Awareness, consequences, emancipation

Flower wisdom for today
What is the greatest
gift you have ever
been given or have
naturally developed?

Birthday flower: Gymea lily people are insightful, ambitious individuals who love to be problem solvers. They have a strong sense of awareness that supports their plans and helps them to easily settle in to most situations in life.

'Awareness is the greatest agent for change.'
ECKHART TOLLE

2 JULY

MORNING GLORY
Ipomoea purpurea
Consistency, mortality, affection

Flower wisdom for today
If you didn't spend time and
energy on small conflicts what
would you do with those assets?

Birthday flower: morning glory people are dependable, emotionally
tough, incredibly warm and considerate. They thrive when caring for other
people and projects and have a great fondness for animals and nature.

*'Consider the lilies of the field whose bloom is brief –
we are as they; like them we fade away as doth a leaf.'*
CHRISTINA ROSSETTI

3 JULY

WHITE CLOVER
Trifolium repens
Unity, strength, observation

Flower wisdom for today
Is there a song or poem
that you feel describes you?
Explore the origins
of this piece and its creation.

Birthday flower: being born under white clover indicates people who are group creators with a deep fondness for record keeping, legacy creation and storytelling. They find their happy place in weaving a strong family unit.

'To acquire knowledge, one must study; but to acquire wisdom, one must observe.'
MARILYN VOS SAVANT

4 JULY

AMERICAN WATERLILY
Nymphaea odorata
Relationships, faith, repair

Flower wisdom for today
Nothing really ends up
at the place it was.
Gravity ensures that
all things move on to a new place.

Birthday flower: American waterlily people usually lead with their hearts but make no mistake: they are tenacious, adaptable individuals who are physically and mentally powerful. They are usually spiritually aware in their own way.

'If we could see the miracle of a single flower clearly, our whole life would change.'
BUDDHA

5 JULY

SWEET PEA
Lathyrus odoratus
Responsibility, comfort, interest

Flower wisdom for today
No one is ever
responsible
until they accept
responsibility.

Birthday flower: those born under sweet pea love cultivating a life touched by the finer side of living. They are happy, generous, loving homemakers who have a keen interest in other people and their desires.

'Interest is the most important thing in life; happiness is temporary, but interest is continuous.'
GEORGIA O'KEEFFE

6 JULY

COWSLIP
Primula veris
Charm, attraction, intent

Flower wisdom for today
Everything and everyone
has an extraordinary element.
Make it your mission
to find it.

Birthday flower: cowslip people are bold and rather intense individuals who are well liked by others. They find creating new projects, businesses, friends – in fact, anything – rather easy and enjoy exploring the extremes of life.

'The secret of attraction is to love yourself. Attractive people judge neither themselves nor others.'
DEEPAK CHOPRA

7 JULY

EGYPTIAN LOTUS
Nymphaea caerulea
Rebirth, creation, imagination

Flower wisdom for today
Today is the day
you will make a new
agreement with yourself.
What will you do for you?

Birthday flower: those born under the Egyptian lotus are artistic, creative people with big dreams and the capacity to make them happen. They love working towards goals even if they have a tendency to drift off plan.

'Awake, arise, or be forever fallen!'
JOHN MILTON

8 JULY

COMMON HOP
Humulus lupulus
Passion, healing, truth

Flower wisdom for today
Create a passion board
by finding images that all
indicate things that drive you
and ignite your spirit.

Birthday flower: common hop people are big-hearted, honest souls who are
expressive in their words, action and style. They are devoted to their values
and ideals and will often find themselves dedicated to the care of others.

'Always listen to your heart; though it's on
your left side, it's always right.'
NICHOLAS SPARKS

9 JULY

BLUE MINK
Ageratum houstonianum
Relaxation, curiosity, soothing

Flower wisdom for today
Make a commitment
to curiosity while silencing your
need to add your opinion.

Birthday flower: with a determination to find meaning and connection in life, blue mink individuals still always make time for the fun and recreational sides of life. They are investigators with a great ability for deep and complex thought.

*'Your ability to generate power is directly
proportional to your ability to relax.'*
DAVID ALLEN

10 JULY

ZINNIA
Zinnia elegans
Humour, receptiveness, playfulness

Flower wisdom for today
What did you
always
find funny
as a child?

Birthday flower: zinnia people naturally find themselves in supportive roles, where they are very happy. They work well with new concepts and are resourceful individuals who have high standards and a great sense of play about them.

'Every child is an artist. The problem is how to remain an artist once he grows up.'
PABLO PICASSO

11 JULY

BAMBOO PALM
Rhapis excelsa
Purification, action, opinion

Flower wisdom for today
Listen to the opinions
of others without having
to express your own
more often than not.

Birthday flower: hard working and with seemingly limitless skills and talents, bamboo palm people get things done fast and well. They are influential and clever and are thought of by others as being very appealing and interesting.

'You are not entitled to your opinion. You are entitled to your informed opinion. No one is entitled to be ignorant.'
HARLAN ELLISON

12 JULY

TURTLEHEAD
Chelone glabra
Clearing anger, progress, commitment

Flower wisdom for today
When you choose kindness
you grow your happiness
to enrich your world
and make new friends.

Birthday flower: turtlehead people are independent and original in their actions and thoughts. They have a self-reliance that seems almost impossible to others and a direct, graceful manner. They love creating improvements.

'Understand yourself and you understand everything.'
SHUNRYU SUZUKI

13 JULY

PEACE LILY
Spathiphyllum wallisii
Nurturance, well-being, opportunity

Flower wisdom for today
What is your favourite
type of clothing or style to wear?
When do you wear it
and how does it make you feel?

Birthday flower: peace lily individuals are serene by nature but nevertheless strong-willed nurturers who take the practice of being whole seriously. They are a mystery to many who cross their paths but are good and true friends to their circle.

....

....

....

....

....

....

....

....

....

....

....

....

....

*'Behind every winter's heart there is quivering spring and
behind the veil of each night there is a smiling dawn.'*
KAHLIL GIBRAN

DRUMSTICKS
Allium sphaerocephalon
Understanding, fascination, counselling

Flower wisdom for today
Nourish the person you are
instead of begging for the one you
probably will never be.

Birthday flower: dedicated and resilient, drumsticks people are wonderful
listeners who have an abundant amount of patience for others. They
are kind, wise and encouraging and possess easy-going natures.

*'An object in possession seldom retains the
same charm that it had in pursuit.'*
PLINY THE ELDER

15 JULY

BUTTON BUSH
Berzelia lanuginosa
Challenges, new situations, influence

Flower wisdom for today
Remember this:
do the right thing
in the right way
at the right time.

Birthday flower: button bush individuals are adventurous souls who are dynamic thinkers and doers. They easily find their way early in life, and with their great eye for accuracy and lust for innovation they often become creators of new ideas.

'We cannot command nature except by obeying her.'
FRANCIS BACON

16 JULY

DRAGON LILY
Zantedeschia spp.
Empowerment, inner strength, passion

Flower wisdom for today
Describe something
beautiful that others
may not see
in your own words.

Birthday flower: dragon lily people are gracefully strong and steady in their actions and planning. They are dependable and courageous and understand the patience required to build anything of purpose. They love to love.

....
....
....
....
....
....
....
....
....
....
....
....

'Strength does not come from physical capacity.
It comes from an indomitable will.'
MAHATMA GANDHI

17 JULY

MINT
Mentha x piperita
Warmth, ambition, virtue

Flower wisdom for today
Take a big dose of
bliss, kindness
and loveliness
and pour it into an open heart.

Birthday flower: mint people are quick to make friends and jump in where they are needed, as well as being great conversationalists with an exciting and inquisitive manner about them. They think big and aim high and are dependable contributors.

*'In the midst of winter, I finally learned that
there was in me an invincible summer.'*
ALBERT CAMUS

18 JULY

CANDYTUFT
Iberis sempervirens
Indifference, assertiveness, self-healing

Flower wisdom for today
Thoughts grow
no matter where
they are planted.
Make yours radiant.

Birthday flower: candytuft people may at first appear somewhat aloof but this is because they are dedicated to getting things right and are great fact gatherers. They are deep thinkers and are steadfast with their personal plans.

'The duty we owe ourselves is greater than that we owe others.'
LOUISA MAY ALCOTT

19 JULY

PERSIAN APPLE
Citrus medica
Grace, control, comfort

Flower wisdom for today
Always accept
and give
directions
gracefully.

Birthday flower: able to create and provide a sanctuary wherever they find themselves, Persian apple people are lovers of the creative arts and have a fine eye for detail and trends. They are loving, warm and expressive in their passions.

'*Grace has been defined as the outward expression
of the inward harmony of the soul.*'
WILLIAM HAZLITT

20 JULY

COCKSCOMB
Celosia argentea
Affection, singularity, activity

Flower wisdom for today
Given total freedom, what would
you do, why and to what end?

Birthday flower: cockscomb people have a warm glow and vibrant
energy that others are naturally drawn to. They are incredibly industrious
and tackle anything they focus on with great exuberance.

*'Affection is responsible for nine-tenths of whatever
solid durable happiness there is in our lives.'*
C.S. LEWIS

21 JULY

PINK SWEET WILLIAM
Dianthus barbatus
Daring, togetherness, inner joy

Flower wisdom for today
Making new friends
takes a special
kind of courage
and brings special joy.

Birthday flower: centre stage is where you usually find pink sweet William people but with an eye to bringing others with them. They love sharing and creating spaces and lives filled with family, friends and fun.

'For great things are not done by impulse, but by a series of small things brought together.'
VINCENT VAN GOGH

22 JULY

ROCK ROSE
Cistus incanus
Acceptance, solidarity, success

Flower wisdom for today
Never burn your bridges.
No doubt you will
have to cross that river
again sometime.

Birthday flower: rock rose people are innovative explorers who have a way of rising over any challenges they face. They can be a little single minded in their approach, but they are trustworthy and enthusiastic and make great advisers.

'The first step in the evolution of ethics is a sense of solidarity with other human beings.'
ALBERT SCHWEITZER

23 JULY

AJUGA
Ajuga spp.
Clarity, discernment, capability

Flower wisdom for today
Is there a recurring
pattern in your life
that you want to change?
What is a first step?

Birthday flower: ajuga people are adaptable and have a way of being able to get to the heart and point of any matter. They are intuitive and inventive and set good examples in balancing structure with original and creative work and thinking.

'Just one great idea can completely revolutionize your life.'
EARL NIGHTINGALE

24 JULY

BANANA
Musa spp.
Revitalisation, excitement,
physical confidence

Flower wisdom for today
What is the best thing
that has ever happened to you?
How did it make you feel
and why?

Birthday flower: banana people usually find themselves in two roles throughout life: they are dedicated to their health and looks but have a sensitive nature towards others and a keen consideration for community.

....

....

....

....

....

....

....

....

....

....

....

....

'A year from now you will wish you had started today.'
KAREN LAMB

25 JULY

BLAZING STAR
Liatris spp.
Radiance, extension, ideals

Flower wisdom for today
If things happen for a reason,
why do you think that is
or why not?

Birthday flower: hard working and independent and with an inspiring leadership quality, those born under blazing star are often found creating new ways of doing things. They are upbeat in nature and optimistic about almost everything.

'It is not the strongest or the most intelligent who will survive but those who can best manage change.'
CHARLES DARWIN

218

26 JULY

WILD HYACINTH
Hyacinthoides non-scripta
Inner growth, transition, symbolism

Flower wisdom for today
What is the most
important thing you
do every day?
Can you do it more
mindfully?

Birthday flower: wild hyacinth people can seem a little mysterious and sensitive but they are purposeful in their approach to life and have a tendency to keep their plans close. They are usually deeply spiritual or dedicated to a purpose in life.

'To everything there is a season; a time to laugh,
a time to cry, a time to live, a time to die.'
ECCLESIASTES

27 JULY

LARKSPUR
Consolida ajacis
Charisma, leadership, enthusiasm

Flower wisdom for today
Leave a postcard
in a public place
with something
inspiring written on it.

Birthday flower: larkspur individuals appear to be good at everything they turn their hands to but their secret is that they have a great enthusiasm for learning and are prepared to do the work. They are influential and well liked.

'There is no personal charm so great as the
charm of a cheerful temperament.'
HENRY VAN DYKE

28 JULY

ROCK TRUMPET
Mandevilla spp.
Focus, order, mental vigour

Flower wisdom for today
If you need help ask for it.
Better to arrive at your
destination a little lighter
than heavy with frustration.

Birthday flower: being a mentor comes naturally to rock trumpet individuals as they have a way of inspiring others with their authoritative demeanour. They are good listeners and are willing to take the time to understand others.

'Reason is not measured by size or height, but by principle.'
EPICTETUS

29 JULY

YELLOW ROSE
Rosa spp.
Friendship, return, loyalty

Flower wisdom for today
What are the qualities
you value most
in your friends, and
why do you think that is?

Birthday flower: yellow rose people are eternal optimists who put their hearts,
bodies and souls into creating strong groups and families. They value loyalty
above all else and are committed to creating better places and situations.

'Wishing to be friends is quick work, but
friendship is a slow ripening fruit.'
ARISTOTLE

30 JULY

RED JASMINE
Plumeria rubra
Forgiveness, belonging, presence

Flower wisdom for today
Be happy
in this moment,
and find home
where you make it.

Birthday flower: red jasmine people are resilient survivors. They
love challenges and have extraordinary mental capabilities and a
delightful way of seeing the best in other people and situations.

*'I long, as does every human being, to be
at home wherever I find myself.'*
MAYA ANGELOU

223

31 JULY

MARSH MARIGOLD
Caltha palustris
Visualisation, wealth, security

Flower wisdom for today
What are you
most connected to, and
does it make you feel safe?
Can you create a better
space for yourself?

Birthday flower: marsh marigold people have a delightful brilliancy about them that is playful but they are also seriously dedicated to creating and building resources of power and finance. They are skilful and tenacious.

'What is now proved was once only imagined.'
WILLIAM BLAKE

AUGUST

1 AUGUST

CALIFORNIA POPPY
Eschscholzia californica
Force, peace, dreams

Flower wisdom for today
How do you
handle the unknown,
and what does this say
about you?

Birthday flower: California poppy people are thoughtful, self-motivated dreamers who are interested in peace and progression. They are warm and independent and have a high level of conscientiousness for others and the world.

'Never give up on what you really want to do. The person with big dreams is more powerful than one with all the facts.'
H. JACKSON BROWN JR

2 AUGUST

WILD PEAR BLOSSOM
Pyrus pyraster
Passion, adaptability, determination

Flower wisdom for today
What is it about you
that makes you different
from everyone else?
What is it that makes you similar?

Birthday flower: setting high targets for themselves is the way of wild pear blossom people; they never give in or give up. They are unafraid of giving anything a go and are quick decision makers who believe in themselves.

'A well-adjusted person is one who makes the same mistake twice without getting nervous.'
ALEXANDER HAMILTON

3 AUGUST

ORANGE GLADIOLI
Gladiolus spp.
Ego, constancy, quests

Flower wisdom for today
Create a friendly competition
to reach your goal
with someone
you trust completely.

Birthday flower: orange gladioli people have a capacity for learning and success that can be thrilling to watch unfold. They are extremely generous and earthy individuals who are attentive to the needs of others as they make their way.

*'Never, for the sake of peace and quiet, deny
your own experience or convictions.'*
DAG HAMMARSKJÖLD

4 AUGUST

SACRED LOTUS
Nelumbo nucifera
Growth, guidance, spirituality

Flower wisdom for today
Make a collection
of objects that you find sacred
and create an everyday
alter of guidance.

Birthday flower: careful, neat and diligent, sacred lotus people make most things look easy but underneath they work incredibly hard to make things happen. They are respectful and refined and have good reasoning power.

'You are a light that will always guide me, a whisper I'll always strain to hear.'
LORA LEIGH

5 AUGUST

WARATAH
Telopea speciosissima
Survival, courage, dignity

Flower wisdom for today
Describe an act of
courage you displayed
and why you
think it was brave.

Birthday flower: waratah people are open hearted and honest and possess an extremely enthusiastic manner that others find rather hard to ignore. They are confident, courageous all-rounders who are highly self-motivated.

'Always be a first-rate version of yourself.'
AUDREY HEPBURN

6 AUGUST

SUNFLOWER
Helianthus annuus
Wellness, strength, assertiveness

Flower wisdom for today
If you could create a class
to help others about the best
things you have learned in life
what would it involve?

Birthday flower: highly likeable and with a disposition that is sunny, warm and delightful, sunflower people are alert, willing and quick minded. They are usually physically strong and have cheerful dispositions and an unshakeable positivity.

....

....

....

....

....

....

....

....

....

....

'Do not let the behaviour of others destroy your inner peace.'
DALAI LAMA

7 AUGUST

FRENCH MARIGOLD
Tagetes patula
Listening, change, secrets

Flower wisdom for today
If there is one thing you could change about your past, what is it and why would that be?

Birthday flower: French marigold people have an amazing ability to understand others and quickly develop connections with an empathy that is true and deep. They are supportive, reliable and magnanimous when things don't go to plan.

'Can you remember who you were, before the world told you who you should be?'
CHARLES BUKOWSKI

8 AUGUST

VALERIAN
Polemonium caeruleum
Accommodation, merit, versatility

Flower wisdom for today
When you choose to enjoy
your life you choose
to be happy anywhere.

Birthday flower: valerian people are easy to talk to and are usually very friendly and considerate. They are sympathetic towards the needs of others and are happy to make room for others in their lives while also being great diplomats.

*'Never set a child afloat on the flat sea of life
with only one sail to catch the wind.'*
D.H. LAWRENCE

9 AUGUST

JASMINE
Jasminum officinale
Abundance, victory, thoughtfulness

Flower wisdom for today
Limiting beliefs block even
the strongest of us.
What are yours?

Birthday flower: jasmine people love creating awareness and sharing information they think others should know. They spend a lot of time fostering meaningful connections and are motivational, passionate and stay true to their ethics.

'Never doubt that a small group of thoughtful, committed citizens
can change the world. Indeed, it is the only thing that ever has.'
MARGARET MEAD

10 AUGUST

TRUMPET CREEPER
Tecoma radicans
Rising above, attractiveness, seduction

Flower wisdom for today
The last thing you hear or see before you go to sleep should be what you want tomorrow to be.

Birthday flower: well rounded and often gifted, those born under trumpet creeper are perfectionists who usually reject the status quo. They do have a strong desire to work above and beyond what is expected and are rather entertaining individuals.

'The reason why we struggle with insecurity is because we compare our behind the scenes with everyone else's highlight reel.'
STEVEN FURTICK

11 AUGUST

PEONY
Paeonia officinalis
Nobility, wealth, healing

Flower wisdom for today
Forget the dream board.
Create a feel-good board
with all the things you love.

Birthday flower: peony people have a huge sense of social responsibility.
They exert a strong personal influence on others, thrive in positions
of power and are usually personally extremely successful.

....
....
....
....
....
....
....
....
....
....
....
....

'If a man be endowed with a generous mind,
this is the best kind of nobility.'
PLATO

12 AUGUST

BERGAMOT
Monarda didyma
Grounding, flexibility, convention

Flower wisdom for today
What is the best advice
you have ever received,
and what changed in your
life because of it?

Birthday flower: bergamot people pay close attention to the important things as they are very good at avoiding distractions. They accept people for who they are and have exceptional manners and style, and they are always ready to help others.

'Since we cannot change reality, let us change the eyes which see reality.'
NIKOS KAZANTZAKIS

13 AUGUST

CAST-IRON PLANT
Aspidistra elatior
Longevity, pride, spiritedness

Flower wisdom for today
The more you believe
in magic the more magical
things will happen.

Birthday flower: cast-iron plant individuals are exceptionally loyal and supportive of the people, places and institutions they are aligned with. They are honourable and trustworthy and believe that the needs of the many outweigh the few.

'It is normal to rise above pride, but you
must have the pride to do so.'
GEORGES BERNANOS

PURPLE CONEFLOWER
Echinacea purpurea
Immunity, wholeness, integrity

Flower wisdom for today
Before you leave your home today,
what is one thought you
can leave behind?

Birthday flower: purple coneflower individuals exert a great influence on others throughout their entire lives. They are confident, self-assured people with big hearts and a graceful trustworthiness that is inspiring to others.

'The ultimate measure of a man is not where he stands in moments of comfort and convenience, but where he stands at times of challenge and controversy.'
MARTIN LUTHER KING JR

15 AUGUST

BURDOCK
Arctium lappa
Healing, persistence, command

Flower wisdom for today
Choose to self-nurture in nature.
Talk a walk in a park or
grow something new.

Birthday flower: polite and considerate while showing great attention to others, burdock people tend to find themselves continually exploring the wonders of the human condition. They are quietly powerful in their demeanour.

'So many of our dreams at first seem impossible, then they seem improbable, and then, when we summon the will, they soon become inevitable.'
CHRISTOPHER REEVE

16 AUGUST

CHIVES
Allium schoenoprasum
Protection, longevity, goals

Flower wisdom for today
Make your
inner voice
the kindest
one you hear.

Birthday flower: being born under the influence of chives indicates people who place a great importance on achieving personal goals and are conscientious in all they decide to align with. They are always willing to help others.

'Goals that are not written down are just wishes.'
FITZHUGH DODSON

17 AUGUST

FUCHSIA
Fuchsia magellanica
True feelings, amiability, versatility

Flower wisdom for today
What is something
you wish you could redo,
and why would it be better
this time around?

Birthday flower: social and gracious and generous in nature, fuchsia people are usually easy-going and great communicators. They are affectionate and passionate about people, places, work and ideas.

'Getting over a painful experience is much like crossing monkey bars. You have to let go at some point in order to move forward.'
C.S. LEWIS

18 AUGUST

DAYLILY
Hemerocallis spp.
Coquetry, flirtation, patience

Flower wisdom for today
You never
have to be perfect
in order to
be amazing.

Birthday flower: daylily people are determined and self-reliant individuals with keenly alert minds. They thrive in difficult situations and have unending patience while being able to adapt to other people and groups quickly.

'If you don't like something change it; if you can't change it, change the way you think about it.'
MARY ENGELBREIT

19 AUGUST

OX-EYE DAISY
Leucanthemum vulgare
Obstruction, surprise, clarity

Flower wisdom for today
What skills
have you gained
from having to
overcome an obstacle?

Birthday flower: ox-eye daisy people can hold positions of great responsibility and have a keen sense of sportsmanship and justice. They are strong minded and never feel at a loss to stand up for a challenge.

*'Mystification is simple; clarity
is the hardest thing of all.'*
JULIAN BARNES

20 AUGUST

PINCUSHION
Leucospermum spp.
Acceptance, discrimination,
inquisitiveness

Flower wisdom for today
Spend time wisely
with good friends,
good books
and good thoughts.

Birthday flower: pincushion people have serene, generous temperaments and are faithful to duty and the care of others. They are curious about life and find fulfilment in research and study.

*'For after all, the best thing one can do
when it is raining, is to let it rain.'*
HENRY WADSWORTH LONGFELLOW

21 AUGUST

GRANADILLA
Passiflora ligularis
Purpose, vision, composure

Flower wisdom for today
Think of a public figure
who inspires you:
what do you
think their values are?

Birthday flower: intelligent and attentive and with a value system that favours positive attitudes and hard work, granadilla people are inspiring to be around and develop great knowledge on the subjects of their passion and focus.

'Purpose is the place where your deep gladness meets the world's needs.'
FREDERICK BUECHNER

22 AUGUST

RED HIBISCUS
Hibiscus rosa-sinensis
Love, desire, imagination

Flower wisdom for today
What is something you
know is true, and
why is that and how
does it guide your life?

Birthday flower: red hibiscus individuals are optimistic and resourceful
and enjoy the mysteries of life and the unknown. They believe anything is
possible and share their fun-loving, curious natures with everyone.

'It is not what you look at that matters, it's what you see.'
HENRY DAVID THOREAU

23 AUGUST

ROSE-SCENTED GERANIUM
Pelargonium graveolens
Poise, harmony, unity

Flower wisdom for today
Describe in
mindful detail
your favourite
personal photograph.

Birthday flower: rose-scented geranium people are consistent, have a high sense of social responsibility and are well organised in their approach. They love raising questions that form the basis of personal exploration.

'He who wants a rose must expect the thorn.'
PERSIAN PROVERB

24 AUGUST

VENUS FLY TRAP
Dionaea muscipula
Preparation, examination, solutions

Flower wisdom for today
If you know you
could not fail,
what is something
you would do right now?

Birthday flower: dependable and with a way of finding effective though unusual ways of doing things, Venus fly trap people are self-disciplined and resourceful. They never wait for things to happen; they make them happen.

'The only real voyage of discovery consists not in seeking new landscapes but in having new eyes.'
MARCEL PROUST

249

25 AUGUST

LAUREL
Laurus nobilis
Victory, merit, energy

Flower wisdom for today
When is your peak energy
power hour, and could you rearrange
your day to better use this time?

Birthday flower: laurel people are outgoing and adventurous individuals
who bounce back quickly from negative experiences. They have an infectious
positivity about them that others find irresistible and are keen team players.

*'Enthusiasm is excitement with inspiration,
motivation, and a pinch of creativity.'*
ROBERT FOSTER BENNETT

26 AUGUST

HOLLYHOCK
Alcea rosea
Ambition, self-containment, optimism

Flower wisdom for today
Say goodbye to your
inner victim.
Make room for your
inner champion.

Birthday flower: seeking out opportunities, training and peers is a lifelong practice for the hollyhock born. They have strong willpower and tackle tasks that others would not dream of attempting while being delightfully cheerful.

'If stars appeared only one night every thousand years, how man would marvel and adore.'
RALPH WALDO EMERSON

27 AUGUST

TUBEROSE
Polianthes tuberosa
Pleasure, intimacy, caring

Flower wisdom for today
Delight in the small,
the fleeting and the sweet
but think and live large,
expansively and bold.

Birthday flower: tuberose individuals always encourage others along their
way and often find themselves as creators of groups and large projects.
They are people-oriented, upbeat folk with strong social skills.

*'Is not this the true romantic feeling – not to desire to
escape life, but to prevent life from escaping you?'*
THOMAS WOLFE

28 AUGUST

NUT TOP
Isopogon anemonifolius
Memory, language, empathy

Flower wisdom for today
Write out a list of positive things
you think you need to hear today.
Read over them throughout your day.

Birthday flower: dedicated to the feelings and even the lives of others, nut top
people are brilliant at seeing what needs to be done and then stepping straight
in. They are determined, eager and respectful and also exceptionally agreeable.

*'We all have empathy. We may not have
enough courage to display it.'*
MAYA ANGELOU

29 AUGUST

NERINE
Nerine spp.
Luck, freedom, structure

Flower wisdom for today
Write down a list
of possible activities
on scraps of paper.
Randomly choose one and do it!

Birthday flower: nerine people usually shun authority and rules and make their own but not in destructive ways. They are trailblazers who value their freedom and free thought and are rather gregarious in personality.

'May we think of freedom, not as the right to do as we please, but as the opportunity to do what is right.'
PETER MARSHALL

30 AUGUST

BORONIA
Boronia spp.
Clarity, reliability, understanding

Flower wisdom for today
What is one thing you would
like more of and one thing
you would like less of?

Birthday flower: boronia people are assertive but will usually give others the benefit of the doubt as they value strong connections. They have cheerful demeanours, are completely reliable and offer information and help freely.

'Everything that irritates us about others can lead us to an understanding of ourselves.'
CARL JUNG

31 AUGUST

TAIL FLOWER
Anthurium andraeanum
Creativity, circulation, integrity

Flower wisdom for today
Think about the most amazing
meal you have ever had
and remember who cooked it.

Birthday flower: tail flower people appear to be always in a good mood
or it's not far from the surface. They are entertaining, relaxed and fun to
be around as they put a lot of importance on social interactions.

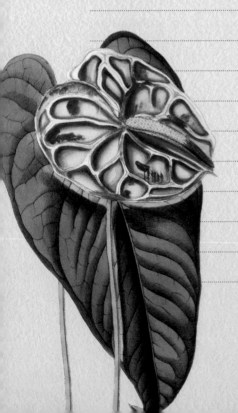

'You are integrity when the life you are living on the
outside matches who you are on the inside.'
ALAN COHEN

SEPTEMBER

1 SEPTEMBER

SYDNEY WATTLE
Acacia longifolia
Joy, optimism, conscientiousness

Flower wisdom for today
This month set one big intention
you have never achieved
and make it happen.

Birthday flower: Sydney wattle people are adventurous and clever individuals with a gift for bouncing back quickly from negative experiences. They are optimistic and highly intelligent and others find them irresistibly charming.

'The greatest barrier to consciousness is the belief that one is already conscious.'
P.D. OUSPENSKY

2 SEPTEMBER

MALLOW BLOSSOM
Malva sylvestris
Warmth, humility, fairness

Flower wisdom for today
Make something for someone
you know and give it to
them for no reason.

Birthday flower: those born under the influence of mallow blossom
are happy to be involved in processes that have the potential to lead to
worthwhile creations. They are kind and thought highly of by their peers.

*'Pride is concerned with who is right. Humility
is concerned with what is right.'*
EZRA TAFT BENSON

3 SEPTEMBER

PINK ASTER
Aster spp.
Making amends, talent, fortitude

Flower wisdom for today
Children and students
should be embraced
for who they are, not what
you want them to be.

Birthday flower: pink aster people tend to wear their emotions on their sleeves but are able to see things in a positive and practical light. They are friendly and trusting and possess a manner of vulnerability that is seen as being honest.

*'Not everything that is faced can be changed, but
nothing can be changed until it is faced.'*
JAMES BALDWIN

4 SEPTEMBER

PAPER DAISY
Rhodanthe spp.
Fortitude, independence, foundation

Flower wisdom for today
What is something you want
to do better right now?
Start a plan; start today.

Birthday flower: never ones to give in to peer pressure, those born under
paper daisy are happy in their own company and exceptionally goal oriented.
They hate wasting time but are known for not being easily upset.

*'What you see in others has more to do with
who you are than who other people are.'*
EPICTETUS

5 SEPTEMBER

DANCING LADY ORCHID
Oncidium flexuosum
Personal growth, imagination, flow

Flower wisdom for today
Take a forest bath
by walking very
slowly among the trees.
Observe and be quiet.

Birthday flower: dancing lady orchid individuals are intellectual and extremely logical. They love education, study and seeking the answers to life's big questions and have a philosophical nature.

'I do not seek. I find.'
PABLO PICASSO

6 SEPTEMBER

FEATHERHEAD
Phylica spp.
Helpfulness, sharing, taste

Flower wisdom for today
What do
you consider
a productive
day looks like?

Birthday flower: those born under the influence of featherhead love making others feel valued and important to them while being fair, non-judgemental and attentive. They are encouraging, warm and helpful and thus well liked.

'Believe one who has tried it.'
VIRGIL

7 SEPTEMBER

YUCCA
Yucca spp.
Planning, perspective, diligence

Flower wisdom for today
All lasting growth and satisfaction
comes from challenging work
that is undertaken with dedication,
not from shortcuts and falsehoods.

Birthday flower: yucca people are engaging with others and love being
involved in discussions and debates. They are knowledgeable in many different
areas and are also confident and determined and have cheeky charm.

*'Everything we hear is an opinion, not a fact.
Everything we see is a perspective, not the truth.'*
MARCUS AURELIUS

8 SEPTEMBER

MYRTLE
Myrtus communis
Love, immortality, seriousness

Flower wisdom for today
Everyone needs to
feel appreciated as
it fills their soul
with love and motivation.

Birthday flower: those born under the influence of myrtle are often found expressing themselves openly with an excitement about their loves and interests that can be intoxicating. They are risk takers who nonetheless plan well.

'The key to immortality is first living a life worth remembering.'
BRUCE LEE

9 SEPTEMBER

FLAME TREE
Delonix regia
Glory, success, introspection

Flower wisdom for today
Be prepared
because success
is always looking
for a place to land.

Birthday flower: flame tree individuals are happy and inspirational and see worth that others miss in people and projects. They are exceptionally open and giving and have a determination for success and self-improvement.

'Progress is impossible without change, and those who cannot change their minds cannot change anything.'
GEORGE BERNARD SHAW

10 SEPTEMBER

SWEET VIOLET
Viola odorata
Steadfastness, loyalty, humility

Flower wisdom for today
What have you learned from
non-fiction and fiction books
and what did you
do with that gift?

Birthday flower: possessing eagerness and delightfully positive attitudes, sweet violet people are devoted friends and co-workers who will always be dependable. They are true in thought and action and are conversational and giving.

'You can easily judge the character of a man by how he treats those who can do nothing for him.'
JOHANN WOLFGANG VON GOETHE

11 SEPTEMBER

GOLDEN RAIN
Laburnum anagyroides
Relationships, connection, nurturance

Flower wisdom for today
Describe something
that smelled good
for you today and
what it reminded you of.

Birthday flower: golden rain people have the ability to apply themselves to the nurturing of their interests so that development is always assured. They are deeply caring and protective individuals with an old-fashioned sweetness.

'Connection gives purpose and meaning to our lives.'
BRENÉ BROWN

12 SEPTEMBER

CHINA PINK
Dianthus chinensis
Inner joy, fearlessness, ethics

Flower wisdom for today
Follow your joy,
and embrace
the sparkle and
share the light.

Birthday flower: with an eye always to diplomacy, China pink people are trustworthy and strong listeners. They remain calm in tough situations and are able to easily direct others to focus on their joy while offering hope.

'It is never too late to be what you might have been.'
GEORGE ELIOT

13 SEPTEMBER

SHOOTING STAR
Dodecatheon meadia
Consciousness, resilience, destiny

Flower wisdom for today
All that you know
anyone can know.
What sets you apart
is how you use your knowledge.

Birthday flower: those born under the influence of shooting star are never swayed by the plans or ideas of others once they have made a resolution. They are assertive and able to face fears without letting go of their values or goals.

'The human capacity for burden is like bamboo – far more flexible than you'd ever believe at first glance.'
JODI PICOULT

14 SEPTEMBER

HAWORTHIA
Haworthia spp.
Effectiveness, prevention, reversal

Flower wisdom for today
Do not hold on
to what you know
has to go
due to habit.

Birthday flower: haworthia people are deeply compassionate and have rock-solid core values that others find comforting. They are eager change-makers who have a great drive to look after the earth, their community and those close to them.

'I've learned that people will forget what you said, people will forget what you did, but they will never forget how you made them feel.'
MAYA ANGELOU

15 SEPTEMBER

FAIRY WAND
Dierama pendulum
Motivation, enchantment, attractiveness

Flower wisdom for today
Meaningful connections
you create are the most
powerful type of magic.

Birthday flower: being born under the influence of fairy wand indicates
highly organised individuals who can get things done quickly and effectively.
They are motivational and proactive and have a quick wit and humour.

*'Our greatest weakness lies in giving up. The most certain
way to succeed is always to try just one more time.'*
THOMAS A. EDISON

16 SEPTEMBER

CHESS FLOWER
Fritillaria meleagris
Depth, steadfastness, competition

Flower wisdom for today
Draw a simple map
of your garden
or the one
of your dreams.

Birthday flower: chess flower people are quick to learn from past mistakes and make changes while generously passing on their experiences to others. They are dependable, eager individuals with a strong, steady influence.

'What can people not accomplish if they will but master the secret of steadfast perseverance.'
ALICE HEGAN RICE

17 SEPTEMBER

SNEEZEWEED
Helenium autumnale
Acceptance, tenaciousness, reliance

Flower wisdom for today
Listen to what your inner
voice says when your
integrity slips.

Birthday flower: those born under sneezeweed are friendly, tolerant and very good at controlling their emotions and have an unending capacity for forgiveness. They are objective and good at putting themselves in other people's shoes.

*'Almost everything will work again if
you unplug it for a few minutes.'*
ANNE LAMOTT

18 SEPTEMBER

CUP AND SAUCER VINE
Cobaea scandens
Excellence, influence, aesthetics

Flower wisdom for today
Did you have an imaginary friend
as a child? If not, create one now
and write a letter to them.

Birthday flower: cup and saucer vine people pay close attention to others and are charming, persuasive individuals who apply themselves completely to their passions. They are good listeners who have confidence and inspire it in others.

'An artist's sphere of influence is the world.'
CARL MARIA VON WEBER

19 SEPTEMBER

GARDEN TICKSEED
Coreopsis tinctoria
Calmness, elegance, pleasure

Flower wisdom for today
What was the most
meaningful gift
you ever received
and why was that?

Birthday flower: calmness and a desire for peace are traits that garden tickseed people value most. They have strong control of their emotions and excellent reasoning skills and are good judges of their own needs and those of other people.

'The time to relax is when you don't have time for it.'
SYDNEY J. HARRIS

20 SEPTEMBER

BURNING BUSH
Dictamnus albus
Reduction, observation, cohesiveness

Flower wisdom for today
You must be willing to look
beneath your own covers
to become self-aware.

Birthday flower: burning bush people always move in positive and purposeful ways towards the future and when coming upon new situations. They assume the best of people and work hard to maintain favourable, happy relationships.

*'If there ever comes a day when we can't be together,
keep me in your heart. I'll stay there forever.'*
WINNIE THE POOH, A.A. MILNE

21 SEPTEMBER

BUTTERFLY WEED
Asclepias curassavica
Relationships, family, progression

Flower wisdom for today
Draw a map of your heart
and put all the things
in it that make it beat.

Birthday flower: those born under the influence of butterfly weed are focused on rewards and are confident in social settings. They are happy stepping outside of their comfort zones and are always moving around or doing something.

'Personal relationships are the fertile soil from which all advancement, all success, all achievement in real life grows.'
BEN STEIN

22 SEPTEMBER

PINCUSHION PLANT
Diapensia lapponica
Bravery, individualism, drive

Flower wisdom for today
Dreams do not always need
a destination but they do need you
to move in its direction.

Birthday flower: pincushion plant individuals are centred and have strong work and personal ethics. They sometimes have a rebellious streak but they are accepting of others, and they place high value on personal freedom and success.

'Fear is the thief of dreams.'
ANONYMOUS

23 SEPTEMBER

PINK HIBISCUS
Hibiscus rosa-sinensis
Self-expression, breakthroughs,
playfulness

Flower wisdom for today
If you had no reference
to how old you are,
think about what age you feel.
Why is that and how does it serve you?

Birthday flower: pink hibiscus people are always prepared for change and alternatives to what they are currently aligned with. They are alert and observant and have good social skills and an attentiveness that is warm and comforting.

'If you obey all the rules, you miss all the fun.'
KATHARINE HEPBURN

24 SEPTEMBER

CHAMOMILE
Matricaria chamomilla
Relaxation, generosity, wandering

Flower wisdom for today
Give more
than you expect.
Share more
than you keep.

Birthday flower: with a mantra of 'working to live, not living to work' as their guide, chamomile people are agreeable, carefree individuals with good senses of humour. They are also exceptionally helpful and thoughtful.

'A good teacher helps you explore the maximum.'
B.K.S. IYENGAR

25 SEPTEMBER

CYCLAMEN
Cyclamen persicum
Withdrawal, childhood
healing, vulnerability

Flower wisdom for today
The greatest gift you can give
to those who are unwell
is your time and your ear.

Birthday flower: cyclamen people treat others the way they would like to be treated and offer grace to those who need it. They are gentle souls with a strong sense of justice and an encouraging manner that others are inspired by.

'Vulnerability is our most accurate measure of courage.'
BRENÉ BROWN

26 SEPTEMBER

LIVERWORT
Hepatica nobilis
Kindness, patience, focus

Flower wisdom for today
Never miss a moment
to speak a kind word,
to breath in beauty and
to listen to truth.

Birthday flower: those born under the influence of liverwort are brilliant at time management and quickly bounce back from setbacks. They are patient, content and peaceful and display an easy-going and likeable character.

'All we have to decide is what to do with the time that is given us.'
GANDALF IN *THE FELLOWSHIP OF THE RING*, J.R.R. TOLKIEN

27 SEPTEMBER

BUSY LIZZIE
Impatiens walleriana
Attention, completion, acceptance

Flower wisdom for today
Walk barefoot
upon the earth;
stand and let
the earth hold you.

Birthday flower: possessing genuine warmth and energy, busy Lizzie people are also attentive individuals who greet all situations as they present themselves. They are generous and have a way of making others feel special.

'Be like a postage stamp. Stick to one thing until you get there.'
JOSH BILLINGS

28 SEPTEMBER

EDELWEISS
Leontopodium nivale
Dedication, bravery, education

Flower wisdom for today
Describe an accomplishment
you are most proud of.
Why do you think
this success matters to you?

Birthday flower: edelweiss people have a well-developed sense of their own purpose and step up to leadership when required. They have forceful convictions, are strong for others and are always willing to put the welfare of others first.

'The beautiful thing about learning is that nobody can take it away from you.'
B.B. KING

29 SEPTEMBER

COCK'S HEAD
Hedysarum coronarium
Vitality, creative energy, intense feelings

Flower wisdom for today
Everything that ignites happiness
begins with a smile.
The outward action of smiling
makes its way within and
becomes a reality.

Birthday flower: cock's head people have exuberance for life, adventurous spirits, strong senses of humour and usually big personalities. They are entertaining and eager and inspire confidence in others.

*'When you do things from your soul, you
feel a river moving in you, a joy.'*
RUMI

30 SEPTEMBER

TREASURE FLOWER
Gazania rigens
Visualisation, truths, capability

Flower wisdom for today
Anything made by a person
who is passionate in their craft
is an object of wisdom
and a gift to the world.

Birthday flower: treasure flower people believe there are always solutions if you look for them. They are determined and cool in the face of challenges and are happy to seek the advice of others. They also possess curious natures and an eagerness to assist.

'The truth is rarely pure and never simple.'
OSCAR WILDE

OCTOBER

1 OCTOBER

DAHLIA
Dahlia pinnata
Encouragement, dignity, resilience

Flower wisdom for today
If you are unhappy
with what you are not getting
it's time to look at
what you are putting in.

Birthday flower: dahlia people have high expectations of themselves and others and they take responsibility, community and connections they make with great seriousness. They are dependable, interactive, grounded and trustworthy.

'All the world is full of suffering.
It is also full of overcoming.'
HELEN KELLER

2 OCTOBER

WILD MARIGOLD
Tagetes minima L.
Stamina, release, acuteness

Flower wisdom for today
Make a declaration
to take it slow
in matters
that matter most.

Birthday flower: being goal oriented and possessing a love of learning as much as possible about the object of their focus, wild marigold people make wonderful mentors. They are passionate perfectionists who are fast to let go of what is not working.

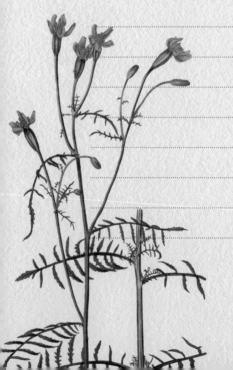

'Let me tell you the secret that has led me to my goal. My strength lies solely in my tenacity.'
LOUIS PASTEUR

3 OCTOBER

PINK CHRYSANTHEMUM
Chrysanthemum x *morifolium*
Well-being, trends, intensity

Flower wisdom for today
Your microbiome affects your mood and behaviour as well as brain function. Regular contact with dirt does wonders so start gardening!

Birthday flower: pink chrysanthemum people have an intensity that leads them to be gifted explorers who are happy to sacrifice in order to achieve. They are direct, organised, productive people who are also deeply caring.

'A healthy attitude is contagious but don't wait to catch it from others. Be a carrier.'
TOM STOPPARD

4 OCTOBER

FLANNEL FLOWER
Actinotus helianthi
Intimacy, forgiveness, trust

Flower wisdom for today
Keeping your word
brings a closeness
to others that no amount
of giving can replace.

Birthday flower: flannel flower people are intensely empathetic and kind believers who treat everyone with a soft gentleness. They usually have few cares as they are quick to forgive and are thoughtful, cheerful and loving.

'Self-trust is the first secret of success.'
RALPH WALDO EMERSON

5 OCTOBER

CUCKOO FLOWER
Lychnis flos-cuculi
Life, restoration, justice

Flower wisdom for today
If you were in charge of your country
what would you change, and what
would you want to stay the same?

Birthday flower: cuckoo flower people are organised and efficient and have astonishing vigour in what they turn their attention to. They are hard working, trustworthy and diligent and have huge hearts and the ability to right wrongs.

*'Where do we even start on the daily walk of restoration
and wakening? We start where we are.'*
ANNE LAMOTT

6 OCTOBER

TULIP TREE
Liriodendron tulipifera
Safety, ancestors, service

Flower wisdom for today
Send a love letter to someone in your
family to let them know they are
loved and safe in your care.

Birthday flower: an ability to see the bigger picture while making balanced
and heart-centred decisions makes tulip tree people endearing to others. They
are family sages who have lovely senses of humour and giving hearts.

'What can you do to promote world peace?
Go home and love your family.'
MOTHER TERESA

7 OCTOBER

CYMBIDIUM ORCHID
Cymbidium spp.
Self-healing, contentment, defiance

Flower wisdom for today
Create art without care.
There is no need to sell,
judge or even share.

Birthday flower: cymbidium orchid people are happy in their own spaces and will go to extraordinary lengths to create perfect environments for themselves and others. They are unique, gracious and usually highly artistic.

'At some point, you gotta let go, and sit still, and allow contentment to come to you.'
ELIZABETH GILBERT

8 OCTOBER

MALTESE CROSS
Lychnis chalcedonica
Centring, faith, romance

Flower wisdom for today
Think of the
last time you
were centred:
what was happening?

Birthday flower: those born under the influence of the Maltese cross are loyal and devoted individuals who are easily adored by others. They are flexible while not losing sight of the heart of a matter and are true romantics who love to love.

'To one who has faith, no explanation is necessary.
To one without faith, no explanation is possible.'
THOMAS AQUINAS

9 OCTOBER

LINSEED
Linum usitatissimum
Recalibration, grace, sensitivity

Flower wisdom for today
Take screen breaks or
hours-long mini breaks
and have a detox day
every now and then.

Birthday flower: linseed people are intensely genuine individuals who
are compassionate in nature and are always champions of other people.
They often need alone time and are gracious, empathetic and caring.

'I can never unlove you. I'll just love you in a different way now.'
PIOLO PASCUAL

10 OCTOBER

OLEANDER
Nerium oleander
Caution, respect, precision

Flower wisdom for today
Remember that
every thought and action
flows from the one
previously made.

Birthday flower: those born under the influence of oleander are deeply intuitive and have a consideration for their plans, work and life that is deliberate and precise. They are influential, courteous and reliable with a discerning taste and manner.

'One of the most sincere forms of respect is actually listening to what another has to say.'
BRYANT H. MCGILL

11 OCTOBER

RED BEGONIA
Begonia spp.
Warning, examination, imagination

Flower wisdom for today
Only real threats
can be managed.
Imagined ones
can only be endured.

Birthday flower: red begonia people are a little slow to trust and they value their privacy, but once you are in their inner circle you will stay there for life. They are deep thinking, practical creators who are highly imaginative and clever.

....

....

....

....

....

....

....

....

....

....

....

....

*'There is no higher or lower knowledge, but one
only, flowing out of experimentation.'*
LEONARDO DA VINCI

12 OCTOBER

BLUEBELL CREEPER
Billardiera heterophylla
Release, renewal, generosity

Flower wisdom for today
Give something away
today and every day
even if it is just a kind word,
idea or helping hand.

Birthday flower: complimentary in tone and open to the ideas and needs of others, bluebell creeper people are thoughtful and interesting individuals who are dedicated to natural balance. They are also outgoing realists.

'For it is in giving that we receive.'
FRANCIS OF ASSISI

13 OCTOBER

WILD THISTLE
Cynara humilis
Respect, clarity, intensity

Flower wisdom for today
Find something
in the street
and write
a short story about it.

Birthday flower: a dedication to the improvement and strengthening of the world they find themselves in, wild thistle people are warriors of the soul who believe that answers can always be found. They are reassuring and resourceful.

'Respect your efforts, respect yourself. Self-respect leads to self-discipline. When you have both firmly under your belt, that's real power.'
CLINT EASTWOOD

14 OCTOBER

CUPID'S DART
Catananche caerulea
Flamboyance, love, growth

Flower wisdom for today
Stop noticing differences
and start celebrating
similarities.

Birthday flower: Cupid's dart people have big personalities, great
social skills and a great love of people. They are optimistic dreamers
who love to test boundaries and have great attention to detail.

'Tell me who you love, and I'll tell you who you are.'
CREOLE PROVERB

PACIFIC DOGWOOD
Cornus nuttallii
Witness, domination, movement

Flower wisdom for today
What do you know about
yourself and your intentions?

Birthday flower: those born under the influence of Pacific dogwood are hard workers with strong moral compasses and are usually good at avoiding negativity. They are confident and disciplined and have self-assured manners.

'Leaders don't create followers; they create more leaders.'
TOM PETERS

16 OCTOBER

BOURBON VANILLA
Vanilla planifolia
Seduction, security, discernment

Flower wisdom for today
Draw a picture
using the letters
of your name
to create something about you.

Birthday flower: bourbon vanilla people prefer to lead rather than follow, surrounding themselves with highly skilled and motivated individuals. They are deeply in tune with their emotions and are sincere, steady and proficient.

'He who knows others is clever; He who knows himself has discernment.'
LAOZI

17 OCTOBER

COMMON VERBENA
Verbena officinalis
Moderation, tolerance, resilience

Flower wisdom for today
You can change the
quality of your life
by changing the quality
of your thoughts.

Birthday flower: respectful and great diplomats, common verbena people are patient individuals who appreciate that everyone they meet has a right to their own views. They are at ease with themselves and are consistent and fair.

'The last thing one knows is what to put first.'
BLAISE PASCAL

18 OCTOBER

TREE MALLOW
Malva arborea
Steadiness, leadership, empowerment

Flower wisdom for today
What beliefs
help you
get through
each day?

Birthday flower: often the first to act and speak, tree mallow people are open and love pushing boundaries and limits. They easily embrace new innovations and have strong convictions, being strong advocates for their beliefs.

....

....

....

....

....

....

....

....

....

....

'There are two ways of spreading light, to be the candle or the mirror that reflects it.'
EDITH WHARTON

19 OCTOBER

BASIL
Ocimum basilicum
Travel, liveliness, harmony

Flower wisdom for today
The approval of others
is a never-ending seesaw.
True success is measured in your heart
wherever it finds itself.

Birthday flower: basil people are attentive and welcoming individuals who are
encouraging of others with warmth and hospitality. They are the first to show
appreciation and join groups and are outgoing, eager and adventurous.

'Nobody can bring you peace but yourself.'
RALPH WALDO EMERSON

20 OCTOBER

YELLOW HIBISCUS
Hibiscus rosa-sinensis
Cheerfulness, enthusiasm,
positive self-image

Flower wisdom for today
No one can learn from other
people's lessons.
You have to go through
that test yourself.

Birthday flower: those born under the influence of yellow hibiscus never shy away from challenges and have unending self-confidence in themselves and their abilities. They are vocally expressive, persuasive and strong team players.

'Knowledge of what is possible is the beginning of happiness.'
GEORGE SANTAYANA

21 OCTOBER

MANDRAKE
Mandragora officinarum
Rarity, singularity, activation

Flower wisdom for today
Stretch your mind and your body:
take ten minutes each day
and stretch to an inspiring podcast.

Birthday flower: mandrake people enjoy solitude and trust in their own intuition completely. They are adept at cutting out negative influences in their lives, are patient and respectful of others and are good at moving on.

'Commitment creates a powerful radiant energy that activates all sorts of "miracles" within and around you.'
SUSAN JEFFERS

22 OCTOBER

AIR PLANT
Tillandsia spp.
Mindfulness, allure, adaptation

Flower wisdom for today
You are never
your experiences.
They may shape you but
only if you allow them to.

Birthday flower: air plant people are flexible, highly organised individuals who have strong, quick decision-making abilities. They are brilliant multitaskers with a high level of empathy and they can keep a cool head in challenging times.

'We cannot direct the wind, but
we can adjust the sails.'
DOLLY PARTON

23 OCTOBER

SPLIT ROCK
Pleiospilos nelii
Endurance, stability, positivity

Flower wisdom for today
Just keep being you.
As long as you are growing
you are not compulsory
and neither is anyone else.

Birthday flower: born under the influence of split rock are friendly, confident souls with big, warm hearts and pleasing personalities. They are hospitable and have kind natures and an attentiveness that others find charming.

'When success is your only option, positivity has to be your only choice.'
GERMANY KENT

24 OCTOBER

PHEASANT'S EYE
Adonis vernalis
Remembrance, perfection, letting go

Flower wisdom for today
Draw a picture
or write a tiny story
about a long-lost
childhood friend.

Birthday flower: pheasant's eye people are thoughtful memory keepers who are good at focusing on the positive aspects of the past and learning from the lessons of the past. They are engaging and careful and have an eye for detail.

....

....

....

....

....

....

....

....

....

....

'Quarrels would not last long if the fault was only on one side.'
LA ROCHEFOUCAULD

25 OCTOBER

ZEBRA PLANT
Aphelandra squarrosa
Management, physical self, moderation

Flower wisdom for today
You need some sunshine.
Take ten minutes every
day to lift your mood and
strengthen your body.

Birthday flower: those born under the influence of the zebra plant have great pride in their work and what they create and are exceptionally good at organising events and systems for others. They are also admirable and curious.

'Take care of your body. It's the only place you have to live in.'
JIM ROHN

26 OCTOBER

JAPANESE WITCH HAZEL
Hamamelis japonica
Awakening, cohesion, wisdom

Flower wisdom for today
Find a happy
story in the news
and write about
how it makes you feel.

Birthday flower: Japanese witch hazel people are alert individuals who are always prepared for the unknown or challenges. They are cautious when first meeting others and have a high level of sensitivity across all of their senses.

'A single event can awaken within us a stranger totally unknown to us.'
ANTOINE DE SAINT-EXUPÉRY

27 OCTOBER

TASSEL FERN
Huperzia spp.
Self-preservation, impulsiveness,
reconciliation

Flower wisdom for today
Your capacity
to heal is
greater than
anyone's ability to hurt.

Birthday flower: tassel fern individuals are naturally charismatic and develop a reputation for being experts in particular matters or those who make things work. They are calm in the face of adversity and are usually skilled debaters.

'If you ever find yourself in the wrong story, leave.'
MO WILLEMS

28 OCTOBER

LUPIN
Lupinus bakeri
Curiosity, awareness, new direction

Flower wisdom for today
Set your compass and go!
Use a pace that enables you
to enjoy the journey, not one so
fast you miss the best bits.

Birthday flower: those born under lupin are intelligent experimenters who love questioning everything in order to find better outcomes and ways to proceed. They are driven by a desire for order and are cool-headed, competent explorers.

'My business is to create.'
WILLIAM BLAKE

29 OCTOBER

BATS IN THE BELFRY
Campanula trachelium
Advocation, subconsciousness,
compassion

Flower wisdom for today
Be willing to
grow with grace
and to change
when validly challenged.

Birthday flower: bats in the belfry people are affectionate and supportive of others and of causes close to their hearts with all of the resources they possess. They are able to sense the needs of others and are encouraging and tender.

'You talk when you cease to be at peace with your thoughts.'
KAHLIL GIBRAN

30 OCTOBER

PUMPKIN
Cucurbita pepo
Inspiration, expression, confidence

Flower wisdom for today
You are stronger than you
were yesterday
and you are ready
for tomorrow.

Birthday flower: those born under the influence of pumpkin are highly ambitious souls who quickly embrace opportunities to learn and grow. They have strong willpower and a high level of pride and always think big.

'Inspiration exists, but it has to find you working.'
PABLO PICASSO

31 OCTOBER

JACARANDA
Jacaranda mimosifolia
Potential, education, attentiveness

Flower wisdom for today
Stop yourself today and ask:
am I fully engaged in this
activity and learning?

Birthday flower: jacaranda individuals are balanced, calm and respectful and usually dedicate themselves to lives of education. They are curious and able to learn quickly and easily find peace and happiness in the world.

*'Learn continually – there's always
"one more thing" to learn.'*
STEVE JOBS

NOVEMBER

1 NOVEMBER

MULLA MULLA
Ptilotus exaltatus
Recovery, expansion, new beginnings

Flower wisdom for today
If you need to apologise for something
then today may be the day.
It's never too late
to mend the past.

Birthday flower: mulla mulla people have deep appreciation for the connections they make with others and their impact on the world. They are dedicated to action for the greater good and are resourceful, gracious and expressive.

'Nothing is permanent in this wicked world – not even our troubles.'
CHARLIE CHAPLIN

2 NOVEMBER

WILLOW
Salix alba
Protection, mindfulness, transformation

Flower wisdom for today
Tomorrow is not the place
you will find the tools
for your new beginning or change.
Today holds all you need.

Birthday flower: methodical and thoughtful, willow people can shape-shift their plans and ideas when needed to better suit their goals while at the same time retaining integrity. They are just, assured and contemplative individuals who keep their word.

'The present moment consists of the past and the future. The secret of transformation is how we handle the present moment.'
THICH NHAT HANH

3 NOVEMBER

FLAME TREE OF WOODS
Ixora chinensis
Preference, wholeness, triumph

Flower wisdom for today
If you had
no commitments
today what
would you do?

Birthday flower: flame tree of woods individuals always put their mental and physical health first and foremost in all they do. They are polite and kind and have an eagerness to explore and expand happiness, not only in their own lives but in those of other people.

'Who looks outside, dreams; who looks inside, awakes.'
CARL JUNG

YELLOW CHRYSANTHEMUM
Chrysanthemum morifolium
Charm, involvement, longevity

Flower wisdom for today
What is one
thing you
no longer
hold to be true?

Birthday flower: yellow chrysanthemum people are agreeable, helpful individuals who love being part of the action. They can compromise and are able to follow direction while possessing a sweet eagerness.

*'Most people never run far enough on their first
wind to find out they've got a second.'*
WILLIAM JAMES

5 NOVEMBER

RESURRECTION LILY
Lycoris squamigera
Transition, revelation, knowledge

Flower wisdom for today
If you had a superpower
what would it be
and what is the first
thing you would do with it?

Birthday flower: resurrection lily people are well-spoken, original thinkers who believe in a combination of intuition and facts to find answers. They can focus intently when needed and are quick witted and personally reflective.

'The important thing is not to stop questioning.'
ALBERT EINSTEIN

SOUTHERN MAGNOLIA
Magnolia grandiflora
Divinity, vigour, fulfilment

Flower wisdom for today
What is the best
thing you ever
learned while
reading a novel?

Birthday flower: with the gift of mental and spiritual resilience no matter what they face, southern magnolia people are always willing to step out of their comfort zone with confidence. They are brave, charming and caring.

*'Just because they're not on your road
doesn't mean they've gotten lost.'*
DALAI LAMA

7 NOVEMBER

MOUNTAIN FLEECE
Persicaria amplexicaulis
Conviction, discovery, strength

Flower wisdom for today
It may take
a little time but
you can create
a wonderful future.

Birthday flower: with a high sense of being doers rather than dreamers, mountain fleece people dedicate themselves to first building strong foundations. They are driven by achievement and have intense though open personalities.

....
....
....
....
....
....
....
....
....
....
....
....
....

'Integrity simply means a willingness not to violate one's identity.'
ERICH FROMM

8 NOVEMBER

PHLOX
Phlox spp.
Agreement, unity, depth

Flower wisdom for today
Make this the day
of completion.
Don't leave
anything undone.

Birthday flower: phlox people are deeply aware of the needs and situations of others and have empowering compassion and consideration. They are courteous, goal driven and attentive with respectful manners.

'Competition makes us faster;
collaboration makes us better.'
NANCY STEIGER

9 NOVEMBER

ROCK CAMPION
Silene rupestris
Temptation, illumination, birth

Flower wisdom for today
When you live
with self-respect
your spirit is free
and your heart unbound.

Birthday flower: rock campion people have excellent senses of timing and open minds to notice new ways of doing things. They are ready to jump into action and treat others with a genuine interest in them and their potential.

'There are two kinds of light – the glow that illuminates, and the glare that obscures.'
JAMES THURBER

10 NOVEMBER

SWEET MOCK ORANGE
Philadelphus coronarius
Expansiveness, ritual, creativity

Flower wisdom for today
Make your journey
your destination;
that way you will always
be happy with where you end up.

Birthday flower: sweet mock orange individuals are spontaneous and expressive people who have a way of bringing anything into the realm of possibilities. They are persistent, expansive planners and thinkers with happy spirits.

'Creativity requires the courage to let go of certainties.'
ERICH FROMM

11 NOVEMBER

FIELD POPPY
Papaver rhoeas
Persuasion, continuance, sacrifice

Flower wisdom for today
What is something
you want to do better,
and will you create the space
to make it happen?

Birthday flower: field poppy people possess endurance and memory retention beyond compare and honourable and genuine dedication to service and even sacrifice. They are responsible, fair people with unbiased sensibilities.

*'To see a world in a grain of sand and heaven in a wildflower,
hold infinity in the palm of your hand, and eternity in an hour.'*
WILLIAM BLAKE

12 NOVEMBER

BALLOON PEA
Sutherlandia frutescens
Community, attraction, admiration

Flower wisdom for today
Describe something
that is beautiful to you
but you have noticed
is not to others.

Birthday flower: confident in their own sexuality and sensuality, balloon pea people
have strong senses of playfulness and fun. They are socially adept and trusted
by those closest to them for their ability to create meaningful connections.

'Alone we can do little; together we can do so much.'
HELEN KELLER

13 NOVEMBER

TIBOUCHINA
Tibouchina elegans
Wisdom, insight, spirituality

Flower wisdom for today
Does your path
and purpose in life
find you or do you find it?
What do you feel?

Birthday flower: tibouchina individuals prefer quieter environments, are exceptionally even tempered and have a deep understanding of the importance of wholeness. They are patient and considerate and can be rather modest.

'Wherever my travels may lead, paradise is where I am.'
VOLTAIRE

14 NOVEMBER

RED FEATHER CLOVER
Trifolium rubens
Energy, consciousness, investigation

Flower wisdom for today
Your understanding
of what something is
only exists in that moment.
It will change as time moves on.

Birthday flower: red feather clover people love taking things apart to investigate how they work, and that includes concepts. They have strong observational skills, are interactive and dedicated and adore new ideas and technologies.

'This is part of human nature, the desire to change consciousness.'
MICHAEL POLLAN

15 NOVEMBER

PINK BEGONIA
Begonia spp.
Warnings, encounters, endings

Flower wisdom for today
If you need something to end tonight write down three things you will do tomorrow to begin the undoing.

Birthday flower: resolute and possessing strong senses of responsibility, pink begonia people are amazing problem solvers who with careful evaluation can take on any opportunity that comes their way. They are determined and faithful.

'Real happiness lies in the completion of work using your own brains and skills.'
SOICHIRO HONDA

16 NOVEMBER

PINK RAIN LILY
Zephyranthes carinata
Reconciliation, balance, effectiveness

Flower wisdom for today
Acceptance is never passive;
it is an action that starts
a movement of change.

Birthday flower: pink rain lily individuals have a way of working up into positions of power with ease and a likeability that helps them stay there. They are reasonable and tactful speakers with gentle humour and loads of respect.

'Harmony makes small things grow; lack of it makes great things decay.'
SALLUST

17 NOVEMBER

RAINBOW PINCUSHION
Mammillaria rhodantha
Wholeness, meditation, diversity

Flower wisdom for today
If you could describe
the meaning of your life
in one sentence
what would that be?

Birthday flower: with an unassuming confidence and a downplaying of their abilities, rainbow pincushion individuals are incredibly talented and prefer to focus on others. They are generous, uplifting and encouraging.

*'Meditation is the tongue of the soul
and the language of our spirit.'*
JEREMY TAYLOR

18 NOVEMBER

TEA
Camellia sinensis
Simplicity, intuition, prosperity

Flower wisdom for today
Cultivate generosity
by practising
small acts
of giving each day.

Birthday flower: tea people can see the potential in everything that crosses their paths and believe in the good of humanity while understanding what needs to be improved. They are visionaries who work hard to leave a legacy.

....

....

....

....

....

....

....

....

....

....

....

'Any intelligent fool can make things bigger and more complex ... It takes a touch of genius – and a lot of courage – to move in the opposite direction.'
E.F. SCHUMACHER

19 NOVEMBER

FLOWERING RUSH
Butomus umbellatus
Grounding, constructiveness, information

Flower wisdom for today
Stop and listen to others
and hear what they are sharing.
Be the second to speak
and the first to listen.

Birthday flower: flowering rush people have an intensely connected demeanour as they can filter out distractions while they are working or are focused on important things. They are strong willed and protective and have strong principles.

'And it's easy to stay grounded. The ground is very close. And we walk on it every day.'
KEANU REEVES

20 NOVEMBER

CROTON
Codiaeum variegatum
Movement, change, rebellion

Flower wisdom for today
You may not always
have opportunities
but you always
have the power of choice.

Birthday flower: croton people are gregarious and highly competitive but they have good natures. They are adventurous seekers with happy eagerness for life who love travel, fun and stimulation, and they are also friendly and chatty.

'Change is not made without inconvenience.'
RICHARD HOOKER

21 NOVEMBER

STAR ANISEED
Illicium stellatum
Sweetness, performance, gracefulness

Flower wisdom for today
Act within your heart.
Speak with kindness
and listen with grace.

Birthday flower: star aniseed people are always willing to show their emotions and believe that things happen for a reason. They are generally positive and will forgive others easily and possess calm, thoughtful, agreeable natures.

'Sometimes we need the salt of tears to remind us how to savour the sweetness of life.'
LYSA TERKEURST

22 NOVEMBER

CELANDINE
Ficaria verna
Communication, clarification, guidance

Flower wisdom for today
What did
someone tell you
that you now
know to be true?

Birthday flower: being born under the influence of celandine indicates individuals who are busy and highly productive and thrive under their own created efficiency. They love planning and seeking out better ways to do things.

'Be mindful of your self-talk. It's a conversation with the universe.'
DAVID JAMES

23 NOVEMBER

RUELLIA
Ruellia solitaria
Acceptance, priorities, hopefulness

Flower wisdom for today
Your highest priority
should be your soul;
everything else
will fall into line.

Birthday flower: ruellia individuals are generous and cooperative and have great capacity to open their hearts to others and trust them. They are warm in their manner, believe in goodwill and enjoy the company of others.

'If it's a priority you'll find a way. If it isn't, you'll find an excuse.'
JIM ROHN

24 NOVEMBER

DANDELION
Taraxacum officinale
Clarity, energy, dreams

Flower wisdom for today
Close your eyes
and wish for a world that
appears perfect to you:
what does that look like?

Birthday flower: dandelion people have big personalities and inspiring and powerful ways of living that are other-worldly and playful. They are trendsetters who have a strong sense of their own identities and positive outlooks.

'Start where you are. Use what you have. Do what you can.'
ARTHUR ASHE

25 NOVEMBER

ENGLISH IVY
Hedera helix
Fidelity, fertility, accomplishment

Flower wisdom for today
If you suddenly increased your wealth
what would you do today and
how could you work towards that?

Birthday flower: English ivy people can grow wherever they are planted and have the gift of not getting upset too easily. They are souls of inner emotional strength and great self-reliance along with being accepting of just about anyone.

'If you don't build your dream, someone will hire you to help build theirs.'
TONY A. GASKINS JR

26 NOVEMBER

WALLFLOWER
Cheiranthus cheiri
Preparedness, uniqueness, endurance

Flower wisdom for today
Are those benefiting
from your success
worthy of being
on your team?

Birthday flower: resourceful and creative problem solvers, wallflower people enjoy quietly working away at projects and problems until they are complete. They are intrigued by fantasy and believe anything is possible.

'Always be a first-rate version of yourself, instead of a second-rate version of somebody else.'
JUDY GARLAND

27 NOVEMBER

CORN COCKLE
Agrostemma githago
Vitality, direction, excitement

Flower wisdom for today
If you cannot decide
on a goal, choose a direction
and get going.
The goal will soon appear.

Birthday flower: corn cockle people love getting involved in just about anything but particularly larger community-based projects. They have endless energy, optimistic outlooks and infectious happiness.

'Happiness is a direction, not a place.'
SYDNEY J. HARRIS

LENTEN ROSE
Helleborus spp.
Sensitivity, resilience, irony

Flower wisdom for today
Do you use being busy
as a way to avoid confronting
aspects of your life?

Birthday flower: Lenten rose individuals are beautifully caring and sensitive and are in sync with the energies of others. They are genuine in their work and actions and have quiet, contemplative natures and brave hearts.

'My barn having burned down; I can now see the moon.'
MIZUTA MASAHIDE

29 NOVEMBER

BLEEDING HEART
Lamprocapnos spectabilis
Detachment, provocation, influence

Flower wisdom for today
Make a list of the people who
have most influenced your life:
what are you living from their gifts?

Birthday flower: being able to physically assist in the development of other people or concepts is a driving force in the lives of bleeding heart people. They are protective, supportive and joyful in manner but are also masters of tough love.

....

....

....

....

....

....

....

....

....

....

....

....

'When it comes to persuasion, emotions usually trump intellect.'
WILL PETERS

30 NOVEMBER

GARDENIA
Gardenia jasminoides
Awareness, messages, defensiveness

Flower wisdom for today
Everything within
you is rooted
to the earth and
branches into the universe.

Birthday flower: gardenia individuals provide wise counsel and mentorship even at a very early age. They are survivalists with strong reasoning skills and a willingness to embrace their own vulnerabilities.

'Every sinner has a future, and every saint has a past.'
OSCAR WILDE

DECEMBER

1 DECEMBER

THORN APPLE
Datura stramonium
Initiation, extroversion, identity

Flower wisdom for today
Quickly sketch
the first thing
you see
behind you.

Birthday flower: with an acute sense of right and wrong and the desire to make a change in the world, thorn apple people are also dependable friends and inspiring role models. They are extremely outgoing in manner and style.

'Be who you are and say what you feel because those who mind don't matter and those who matter don't mind.'
BERNARD BARUCH

2 DECEMBER

ICELAND POPPY
Papaver nudicaule
Receptivity, integration, forcefulness

Flower wisdom for today
You probably don't need
to awaken if your
eyes are open;
just take a second look.

Birthday flower: Iceland poppy people are deeply respectful, reliable and socially conscious and have highly cooperative natures. They are industrious and friendly and have a comforting sincerity.

'Force has no place where there is need of skill.'
HERODOTUS

POINSETTIA
Euphorbia pulcherrima
Appreciation, feelings, innovation

Flower wisdom for today
Do you have strong
feelings for a personal possession
that is of no monetary value?
Describe it and why you feel this way.

Birthday flower: poinsettia people adhere mostly to commonly held beliefs and ideas while expressing sound judgement themselves. They are understanding and protective individuals who have a calming presence and grounded attitudes.

'Acknowledging the good that you already have in your life is the foundation for all abundance.'
ECKHART TOLLE

4 DECEMBER

<table>
<tr><td>

HOLLY
Ilex aquifolium
Ingenuity, cheerfulness, homemaking

</td><td>

Flower wisdom for today
The colours you surround
yourself with affect your mood.
Is it time for a colour
facelift at your place?

</td></tr>
</table>

Birthday flower: always resourceful and possessing the ability to assess any
situation quickly, holly people almost always maintain positive outlooks. They
are thrifty and clever and nostalgic about places and their own experiences.

'The best substitute for money is ingenuity.'
PATTI PAGE

5 DECEMBER

ROSELLA FLOWER
Hibiscus sabdariffa
Love, boldness, openness

Flower wisdom for today
All the things you
surround yourself with
will never be as wonderful
as who you surround with your arms.

Birthday flower: rosella flower people are highly logical and rational and have strong listening skills and awareness of their own weaknesses and challenges. They are able to understand the viewpoints of others with a caring heart.

'Love is not only something you feel, it is something you do.'
DAVID WILKERSON

6 DECEMBER

RED CAMELLIA
Camellia japonica
Desire, longing, confidence

Flower wisdom for today
Don't listen
to losers.
Talk with
those who succeed.

Birthday flower: red camellia people are sensuous, love to indulge their senses and are highly aware of the emotions of those around them. They live for the moment and adore surprises, adventures and taking their time.

'As is our confidence, so is our capacity.'
WILLIAM HAZLITT

7 DECEMBER

SPIDER ORCHID
Arachnis flos-aeris
Creativity, difference, purpose

Flower wisdom for today
Which character from
a book, TV show or movie
do you think is most like you
and why is that?

Birthday flower: spider orchid people usually deliberately do things to make them stand out; in reality, they can't help their quirkiness. They are open-minded, confident and highly independent people with a lust for life.

*'It is not our differences that divide us. It is our inability
to recognise, accept and celebrate those differences.'*
AUDRE LORDE

8 DECEMBER

STATICE *Limonium* spp. Stillness, adaptation, commitment	**Flower wisdom for today** You must honour any commitments you made to yourself. Learn to adapt when necessary but always be true to yourself.

Birthday flower: statice individuals are steady and cautious and are always in for the long haul with whatever they do. They are patient and clear sighted and have excellent memories and deep curiosity for the world around them.

'Within you there is a stillness and a sanctuary which
you can retreat at any time and be yourself.'
HERMANN HESSE

9 DECEMBER

ELDER
Sambucus nigra
Fortitude, recovery, resilience

Flower wisdom for today
What is right
for you is spoken
in little tugs
of conscious all day long.

Birthday flower: elder people are deeply studious and dedicate their lives to learning and strengthening their minds, bodies and souls. They are usually pillars of their communities, family or workplaces and are sage in manner.

*'I know of no higher fortitude than stubbornness
in the face of overwhelming odds.'*
LOUIS NIZER

10 DECEMBER

ROSE MALLOW
Lavatera trimestris
Options, humility, ventures

Flower wisdom for today
Each hour today reflects on how
your mood is affecting
what you are doing
and who you are with.

Birthday flower: rose mallow people have almost ferocious manners in their desire to protect others and believe no one can be too careful. They are amazing resource creators and savers and touch the hearts of all they meet.

*'Don't ever take a fence down until
you know why it was put up.'*
ROBERT FROST

11 DECEMBER

FLAMING KATY
Kalanchoe blossfeldiana
Endurance, friendship, ferocity

Flower wisdom for today
Pick a flower that represents
each of your friends.
Arrange them in a circle of tiny vases
to focus your attention on this blessing.

Birthday flower: highly considerate and placing huge importance on friendships and social circles, flaming Katy people are attuned to their environments and responsibilities. They are inspirational and have a strong sense of fairness.

*'What draws people to be friends is that they
see the same truth. They share it.'*
C.S. LEWIS

12 DECEMBER

CREPE MYRTLE
Lagerstroemia spp.
Eloquence, progression, presence

Flower wisdom for today
Plan your life.
If you don't,
someone else
will do it for you.

Birthday flower: crepe myrtle people have a graceful control that makes them commanding presences to those around them. They have high expectations but understanding natures and forgiving souls.

'Time is the wisest counsellor of all.'
SENECA

13 DECEMBER

CROWN OF THORNS
Euphorbia milii
Self-forgiveness, abundance, attention

Flower wisdom for today
Was there a time you failed
and were angry with yourself?
Go back to that time and be kind,
compassionate and positive.

Birthday flower: crown of thorns people have the ability to always say and do the right thing no matter the situation. They are usually successful, confident, have a subtle sense of humour and chose to never dwell on the negative.

'Some people walk in the rain; others just get wet.'
ROGER MILLER

14 DECEMBER

DUSTY MILLER
Silene coronaria
Vision, originality, grit

Flower wisdom for today
Live life
as an exclamation,
not an
explanation.

Birthday flower: being able to always carry themselves with confidence, dusty miller individuals are well read, highly sociable and delightfully original. They are rather debonair and love engaging in conversation.

It is better to fail in originality than to succeed in imitation.'
HERMAN MELVILLE

15 DECEMBER

LILY OF THE FIELD
Sternbergia lutea
Guidance, resourcefulness, creation

Flower wisdom for today
No one who
has a big garden
or a community garden
is ever bored.

Birthday flower: lily of the field people are brilliant, highly organised time managers who can create structure and usually success out of anything they turn their hands to. They are eloquent, driven and enterprising.

'If you change the way you look at things, the things you look at change.'
WAYNE DYER

16 DECEMBER

BETHLEHEM SAGE	Flower wisdom for today
Pulmonaria saccharata	If you are always at war
Breathing, duality, discovery	with your past
	your future
	becomes the victim.

Birthday flower: those born under the influence of Bethlehem sage are introspective and enjoy putting areas of their lives in boxes so they can devote full attention on each as necessary. They are interesting and deep and rather original.

'You are only as free as you think you are and freedom will always be as real as you believe it to be.'
ROBERT M. DRAKE

17 DECEMBER

ALPINE SQUILL
Scilla bifolia
Revitalisation, healing, ease

Flower wisdom for today
Excuse yourself
gracefully
when in the presence
of a gossip.

Birthday flower: alpine squill individuals are composed and goal focused and able to entertain and occupy themselves. They are elegant and graceful under pressure and always make space for others in their lives.

'The reason why we struggle with insecurity is because we compare our behind the scenes with everyone else's highlight reel.'
STEVEN FURTICK

18 DECEMBER

WHITE CAMELLIA
Camellia japonica
Divinity, kindness, authenticity

Flower wisdom for today
True friends are
a link with your past
and a guiding partner
to your future.

Birthday flower: with a desire to lead and an ability to act appropriately no matter the situation, white camellia people are also articulate and adaptable. They maintain their emotions well and always follow through on their word.

'I believe divinity is within us.'
LILLETE DUBEY

19 DECEMBER

SINGAPORE ORCHID
Dendrobium spp.
Flexibility, sexuality, uniqueness

Flower wisdom for today
Don't keep doing
things the same way.
Try a different angle
and then take a leap.

Birthday flower: Singapore orchid individuals are adaptable and have powerful intuitions and a strong sense of the importance of preparation. They are survivalists and achievers with quirky, fun personalities.

'The boldness of asking deep questions may require unforeseen flexibility if we are to accept the answers.'
BRIAN GREENE

20 DECEMBER

IMMORTELLE
Xeranthemum annuum
Eternal love, forgiveness, cheerfulness

Flower wisdom for today
What can you
do today to become
the person
you want to be?

Birthday flower: with a love of exploration and making new discoveries and the ability to let go of that which they cannot change, immortelle people are active, motivated and fun. They are also animated and free spirited.

'I'm sure that love exists, even infinite, eternal love.'
KYLIE MINOGUE

21 DECEMBER

CHRISTMAS CACTUS
Schlumbergera truncata
Intimacy, confidence, togetherness

Flower wisdom for today
You can never
let what is easy
stop you from
doing what is right.

Birthday flower: Christmas cactus people always speak up for what they believe in and align themselves quickly with like-minded individuals and organisations. They are determined and extremely capable.

....

....

....

....

....

....

....

....

....

....

....

....

'Great things are done by a series of small things brought together.'
VINCENT VAN GOGH

22 DECEMBER

BUTTERFLY BUSH
Buddleja curviflora
Rebirth, peacefulness, unveiling

Flower wisdom for today
Every person
you meet
is either
a blessing or a lesson.

Birthday flower: butterfly bush people have great powers of observation and insight and seem to always notice things that others somehow miss. They are solution seekers and peacemakers and are expressive in their manners and style.

'It is not the mountain we conquer but ourselves.'
EDMUND HILLARY

23 DECEMBER

MOUNTAIN DAISY
Ixodia achillaeoides
Support, inner child, freedom

Flower wisdom for today
Treasure your humanity
and that of others.
It will be all you need
if all else is lost.

Birthday flower: with helpful and highly generous natures, mountain daisy people seek opportunities where others are usually fearful to tread. They have light-hearted and encouraging manners they share freely with everyone.

'Never reach out your hand unless you're willing to extend an arm.'
ELIZABETH FULLER

24 DECEMBER

HAWTHORN
Crataegus monogyna
Openness, courage, energy healing

Flower wisdom for today
Commit yourself
to a cause
that is
greater than yourself.

Birthday flower: hawthorn people have great empathy and believe the motivations of others are usually good. They are cheerful in their demeanour and have agreeable natures and kindness for others that is exceptional.

'The way to love anything is to realise that it may be lost.'
G.K. CHESTERTON

25 DECEMBER

STAR FLOWER
Ornithogalum arabicum
Trauma reduction, identity, nurturance

Flower wisdom for today
Spend your time
as carefully
and wisely as
diamonds and gold.

Birthday flower: those born under the influence of star flower are watchful, highly observant individuals who are broad-minded and meticulous planners. They are dedicated healers with strong senses of responsibility.

'Our souls cannot be forced to grow, but like flowers, our spiritual selves can be nurtured until they blossom and flourish.'
JAMES VAN PRAAGH

26 DECEMBER

RANUNCULUS
Ranunculus asiaticus
Inspiration, creativity, charm

Flower wisdom for today
Photograph the first letter
of your name
wherever you find
it all day and make a collage.

Birthday flower: ranunculus individuals are colourful, bright, highly imaginative and very much focused on the here and now. They are playful, enjoy adventure and games and have big, warm, considerate hearts.

'There is no charm equal to tenderness of heart.'
EMMA, JANE AUSTEN

27 DECEMBER

LILY OF THE VALLEY BUSH
Pieris japonica
Worthiness, innocence, purity

Flower wisdom for today
When you get
out of your own way
you will be surprised
at what you find.

Birthday flower: with a lovely sweetness and accepting personalities, lily of the valley bush people are quietly social and have forever-youthful attitudes and huge curiosity for the world. They are studious and are happy in their own company.

'Know your worth. Then add tax.'
ANONYMOUS

28 DECEMBER

FRANGIPANI
Plumeria alba
New life, gracefulness, creativity

Flower wisdom for today
Practise gratitude daily:
write thank you letters,
praise workers
and offer compliments.

Birthday flower: frangipani people are creative freedom seekers who
are accepting of what it takes to succeed and get where they plan to go.
They have patience and persistence and considerate natures.

'Courage is grace under pressure.'
ERNEST HEMINGWAY

29 DECEMBER

ERICA
Erica spp.
Admiration, independence, gratitude

Flower wisdom for today
Being grateful for what has been
strengthens your heart.
Being grateful for what
may be strengthens hope.

Birthday flower: being able to think quickly and accept the challenges of difficult situations means that erica people are usually unflappable. They are resourceful and diligent and possess ways of making others feel secure and safe.

....
....
....
....
....
....
....
....
....
....
....
....

*'Enjoy the little things, for one day you may look
back and realize they were the big things.'*
ROBERT BRAULT

30 DECEMBER

PINEAPPLE LILY	Flower wisdom for today
Eucomis comosa	If you can't
Shift, co-creation, family	give your best
	never expect
	the best.

Birthday flower: pineapple lily individuals are hospitable and spontaneous and choose unique paths in life. They are expressive risk takers who thrive in situations they allow to occur naturally and are easy-going and enthusiastic.

'"Ohana" means family and family means
nobody gets left behind or forgotten.'
STITCH, LILO AND STITCH

31 DECEMBER

SPIDER FLOWER
Cleome spinosa
Vibration, empathy, adaptability

Flower wisdom for today
Learn how to
be happy
when you
are alone.

Birthday flower: spider flower people are focused on their higher selves and often find themselves in positions of spiritual learning or teaching. They are charitable, deeply loving, bright individuals who others are naturally drawn to.

'Those who bring sunshine to the lives of others cannot keep it from themselves.'
J.M. BARRIE

ABOUT THE AUTHOR

Cheralyn Darcey is an ethnobotanist, botanical history author and artist who has written 20 internationally published botanical and gardening titles. A volunteer community garden curator, she creates the gardening designs, systems and education at SWAMP (Sustainable Wetlands Agricultural Makers Project) on the Central Coast of New South Wales.

Cheralyn also produces and hosts a live weekly two-hour gardening radio show *At Home with the Gardening Gang* on *COASTFM963* and writes the weekly *Down in the Garden* page for Central Coast newspapers *Coast News* and *The Coast Chronical* and Newcastle's *Novo News*.

facebook.com/cheralyn.darcey
instagram.com/cheralyn/
cheralyndarcey.com

A Rockpool book
PO Box 252
Summer Hill
NSW 2130
Australia

rockpoolpublishing.com
Follow us! **f** **◎** rockpoolpublishing
Tag your images with #rockpoolpublishing
ISBN: 978-1-925924-69-5

Published in 2022 by Rockpool Publishing

Design by Sara Lindberg, Rockpool Publishing
Edited by Lisa Macken

A catalogue record for this
book is available from the
National Library of Australia

Printed and bound in China
10 9 8 7 6 5 4 3 2 1